D0232627

Counselling
Difficult
Clients

PROFESSIONAL SKILLS
FOR COUNSELLORS

The *Professional Skills for Counsellors* series, edited by Colin Feltham, covers the practical, technical and professional skills and knowledge which trainee and practising counsellors need to improve their competence in key areas of therapeutic practice.

Titles in the series include:

Medical and Psychiatric Issues for Counsellors
Brian Daines, Linda Gask and Tim Usherwood

Personal and Professional Development for Counsellors
Paul Wilkins

Counselling by Telephone
Maxine Rosenfield

Time-Limited Counselling
Colin Feltham

Client Assessment
Stephen Palmer and Gladeana McMahon (eds)

Counselling, Psychotherapy and the Law
Peter Jenkins

Contracts in Counselling
Charlotte Sills (ed.)

Long-Term Counselling
Geraldine Shipton and Eileen Smith

Counselling Difficult Clients

Kingsley Norton and Gill McGauley

SAGE Publications
London • Thousand Oaks • New Delhi

LONGWOOD COLLEGE LIBRARY
FARMVILLE, VIRGINIA 23901

BF
637
.C6
N67
1998

© Kingsley Norton and Gill McGauley 1998

First published 1998

All rights reserved. No part of this publication may be reproduced, stored in a retrieval system, transmitted or utilized in any form or by any means, electronic, mechanical, photocopying, recording or otherwise, without permission in writing from the Publishers.

SAGE Publications Ltd
6 Bonhill Street
London EC2A 4PU

SAGE Publications Inc
2455 Teller Road
Thousand Oaks, California 91320

SAGE Publications India Pvt Ltd
32, M-Block Market
Greater Kailash – I
New Delhi 110 048

British Library Cataloguing in Publication data

A catalogue record for this book is available from the British Library

ISBN 0 8039 7673 9
ISBN 0 8039 7674 7 (pbk)

Library of Congress catalog card number 97–069349

Typeset by Mayhew Typesetting, Rhayader, Powys
Printed in Great Britain by Biddles Ltd, Guildford, Surrey

LONGWOOD COLLEGE LIBRARY
FARMVILLE, VIRGINIA 23901

Contents

Preface		vi
Acknowledgements		xi
1	The Counselling Transaction	1
2	The Influence of Past Interactions	15
3	Counselling Transactions in Context	32
4	Assessment for Counselling	44
5	Practical Points: from Beginning to End	65
6	Preserving Respective Roles	86
7	Restoring the Public–Personal Equilibrium	102
8	Utilizing Contextual Influences	122
9	Interface with Other Models	134
References		147
Index		150

LONGWOOD LIBRARY

1000303918

Preface

Difficulties with clients may surface obviously and dramatically. While some may be present from the outset, others take some time to become apparent. Sometimes a counsellor (or comparable practitioner working in social work, probation, psychiatric or other settings) will label a client as 'difficult', out of a sense of frustration. If so, this tends to locate the difficulty firmly on the client's shoulders. Having been labelled thus, many clients then perform or continue to perform their complementary role as the 'difficult' party with ease – an ease that comes with years of repetition and rehearsal. This is particularly true of clients whose long-standing personality difficulties have contributed to their presenting problems. Such personality difficulties may then frustrate the very process of counselling and the counselling itself becomes part of the client's problem rather than its solution (Lockwood, 1992).

An important therapeutic task, therefore, is for you to avoid such unhelpful labelling of clients, since this process serves to distance you from them, making any accurate empathic connection almost impossible. To avoid this, or to undo it once it has happened, requires an understanding of how stigmatic labels are generated. Based on the personal characteristics of the individual counsellors and their social and professional context, such labels tend to be idiosyncratic. Thus, your difficult client may share some characteristics with the difficult client of another counsellor but is unlikely to share all of them. Use of the label, since it has no generally agreed definition, does not facilitate a dialogue between counsellors or between supervisee and supervisor. You are thus not only emotionally divorced from your client by the process of labelling, but your terminology fails to aid communication with professional colleagues who might otherwise be able to offer support or advice.

To have a useful dialogue about difficulties encountered professionally, whether or not stigmatic labelling is involved, requires a deeper understanding of the origins of any difficulty you experience with your clients. In this book the method described and applied to understanding such difficulties therefore focuses on the *interaction* between counsellor and client, rather than on a search for the origin of difficulty solely within the client. In large measure, the difficulty is thus addressed as arising from and existing within the transaction between you and your client.

The term *counselling transaction* is used to refer to the overall counsellor–client interaction as it implies an active and negotiated interchange between counsellor and client and hints at a partnership which can, in certain respects, be equal. Some readers might infer from the commercial and business usage of the term that we view the counselling transaction as particularly goal-oriented or driven by mercenary motives. This is *not* our view. For us, the term counselling transaction is neutral and suggestive of an appropriate degree of professionalism. The term transaction can also be used to embrace two levels of interaction between you and your client, which can be usefully differentiated in order to analyse the professional relationship and understand it more thoroughly.

The first level of interaction reflects the goal-directed activity which is implicit in your respective roles as counsellor and client. These roles are largely prescribed by the society in which the counselling takes place and tend to be static, although they may be subject to cultural variation. This level of interaction is referred to as 'public'. Intrinsic to this *public level interaction* of role-taking is the professional role of the counsellor and the complementary part played by the client. Aspects of the client's role overlap with those of the 'sick role' (Parsons, 1951). This involves an obligation to seek and accept help and to give up the role once the reasons for its adoption cease to exist. Ideally, you and your client perform your respective roles with a clear focus on mutually agreed therapeutic goals. Obviously some situations, in which counselling is undertaken, are not ideal and will involve statutory responsibilities for the professional concerned and some degree of compulsion to undergo counselling for the client, for example in some probation or social work settings.

In some counselling, the public level work is hard to do since the problems presented are not easy to clarify because they represent deep-rooted maladaptive aspects of the client's personality (sometimes amounting to a psychiatric diagnosis of personality disorder – see Chapter 9). Therapeutic and lasting change may therefore be problematic to establish. In other instances, aspects which derive from the interaction of the personalities of yourself and your client can dramatically erupt into the public level or else insidiously undermine the process of counselling. Where the involvement of the counsellor is part of a statutory duty or where the client is compelled to accept counselling, the therapeutic work can be exceedingly problematic.

The second level of interaction is interpersonal. This *personal level interaction* may sometimes appear to be static. However, it is composed of a rapid and complex interplay of myriad verbal and non-verbal behaviours, many of which you and your client are unaware of. It can dominate or undercut the whole counselling transaction so that the public level activity of achieving the therapeutic goals is deprived of its sustaining interpersonal energy and no productive work is possible. In such a situation, it is as if the personal level interaction is both more powerful and more stable than that of the public level. Achieving unstated and covert personal goals may well be incompatible with the successful attainment of transaction goals which have been overtly agreed.

Counselling transactions are of two sorts – *straightforward* or *complicated* (after Norton and Smith, 1994). These terms do not, however, bear on the degree of complexity of your client's presenting problems nor on the presence of any associated psychosocial difficulties. 'Complex' or 'severe' cases can proceed with a smooth, albeit arduous, course. On the other hand, therapeutic endeavours which initially appear 'simple' can end in failure. At any time in a particular counsellor–client interaction, therefore, either the straightforward or the complicated form can be in the ascendance. The counsellor thus bears in mind this central idea and endeavours to determine whether, at a given point, the transaction is straightforward or complicated.

In practice, minor or transient departures from the straightforward form are not significant, such as short periods during which your clients are regularly late for their appointments with you or when they, in other ways, do not comply with your expectations of them. These may even add zest to the therapeutic endeavour. Beyond a certain point, however, departures become significant and begin to erode the overall therapeutic process, and need to be identified as such. This does not require a heavy-handed or judgemental approach, since such a development is not a crime! Rather, evidence of significant departures can alert you to a potentially serious development within either or both levels of your interaction and, depending upon the particular details of the transaction, it may be necessary for you to intervene actively.

In order to preserve the straightforward transaction, which is relatively fragile, a combination of approaches is required. In essence there are two strategies. The first is to enhance and strengthen the public level interaction by educating your clients about your expectations of them and, implicitly or explicitly, also about the limits to your counselling expertise, thereby encouraging more realistic expectations of you. The second is to identify the existence of personal level activity which does not support and may undermine or supplant the public level and to deal with it. An example of the latter might be raising at the public level interaction, as part of that agenda, your observation that a client appears to be regarding you erotically, as a potential partner rather than as a professional carer.

Attending to both public and personal level interactions can be emotionally and intellectually draining but it can also be rewarding, when it clarifies how the transaction has become complicated and guides you in how to deal with such complication. Monitoring the counselling transaction, by evaluating its public and personal level interactions, can lead to the speedier identification of departures from the straightforward, thereby lessening the likelihood that it becomes complicated. The result of such monitoring can also inform your interventions by providing a systematic and methodical approach to returning the straightforward transaction from the complicated.

The early chapters of this book (Chapters 1, 2 and 3) are devoted to developing the counselling transaction model in detail, drawing also on attachment theory (Bowlby, 1969) and systems theory (von Bertalanffy, 1973). Although we have tried to avoid unnecessary technical language and psychological jargon, we have had to introduce terms of our own, namely the *straightforward* and *complicated counselling transaction*; *public* and *personal level interactions*; *public–personal equilibrium*; and what we consider to be three *basic interaction patterns*, which underlie many of the complicated counselling transactions.

The counselling transaction model is applied to the assessment of the client (Chapter 4), as this allows a crucial opportunity to predict and avoid some later difficulties resulting in a complicated transaction. The model is then used to demonstrate how it can enliven the relatively mundane practical aspects of counselling work (Chapter 5), since it generates a conceptual framework to guide your therapeutic attention and so produce change in your actual practice. Building on earlier chapters (especially on Chapters 1 and 2), this section leads into the final part of the book which, again using the model, introduces intervention strategies to prevent significant departures or to restore the straightforward transaction (Chapters 6 and 7).

A view of the counselling transaction within its wider context (linking closely with the content of Chapter 3) follows. Recognizing the inter-dependence of the counselling transaction and its interpersonal and social environment, interventions are envisaged which include the use of resources external to the counselling relationship itself (Chapter 8). In the last chapter, we consider how some aspects of the model interface with those of other models and how far the different approaches can complement one another.

Throughout the book we have referred continually to six counsellors and clients, whose real names have been changed and identities disguised. We have adopted this method to illustrate how the counselling transaction model translates into actual practice and to demonstrate both the range and subtlety of complicated counselling transactions. The examples, each deliberately partial and brief, slowly build into more complete counselling transactions. This we have considered necessary because unlike a text dealing with the counselling of a specific client group (such as those who misuse drugs or with a specified problem, such as violence), this book attempts to deal with 'difficulty', an aspect which can be elusive and which is exquisitely individual to each counsellor. In order to add variety to the text we use the terms therapy and counselling interchangeably.

Acknowledgements

Many have helped us to write this book – friends, family, former clients and patients. Many cannot be named and formally thanked and will never know how they have informed and influenced our own professional practice. We, nonetheless, owe them a great debt of gratitude, which we wish to acknowledge.

Two members of our respective families merit open and special recognition since they have given their time to read drafts of the manuscript and, even more generously, allowed us to take up, in writing the book, time that otherwise would have been spent with them. We thank Jane and Tim in this respect. Each has contributed enormously to the finished product, whose remaining imperfections are solely our own.

Friends have given of their free time to read parts of earlier drafts of the manuscript and to make helpful and constructive criticisms. In particular, our thanks go to Dr Sam Smith. He was not only generous in his comments but his ideas about transactions and transaction 'windows' helped to form the foundation of much of the thinking that is central to this book.

There are people within the wider systems of Henderson Hospital, Broadmoor Hospital Authority and St George's Hospital Medical School who also deserve a special thanks for helping us in various ways, direct and indirect. In particular, they include Dr Margaret Orr, Dr Nigel Eastman, Dr Chris Evans and the staff team at Henderson Hospital.

We wish to record our thanks and indebtedness to Colin Feltham whose quiet, supportive editorial presence and well-timed prompts have helped us in the writing of this book.

Finally, we wish to thank Julia, Sally and Anne who, apparently untiringly, typed draft after draft, without a hint of complaint. They have enabled us to communicate ideas which we hope will be helpful.

1

The Counselling Transaction

Sheila was an emaciated woman in her late twenties who was persuaded by her brother to seek help for her long-standing eating problems. When the counsellor fetched her from the waiting area for the initial assessment interview, Sheila followed to the consulting room door but did not go in. Feeling awkward and somewhat embarrassed, the counsellor sat down and she spent the next five minutes persuading Sheila to enter. Subsequently, the interview continued as falteringly as it had begun. Sheila maintained that her only motivation for coming to 'therapy' was to placate her brother.

Counselling some clients can be problematic from the outset. Sheila's initial failure to enter the same room as her counsellor could tempt the latter to construe her as 'difficult'. To do so would be understandable. However, such a construction and labelling of Sheila would not help an understanding of her nor inform subsequent counselling interventions.

Labelling a client as 'difficult' may ease the counsellor's feelings of frustration, but, it impairs empathic contact with the client and does not aid communication with a supervisor about the difficulty. Most importantly, it ignores the potential part played by the counsellor in what is essentially a difficult *interaction*. Reframing the client as 'resistant' or 'challenging' rather than 'difficult', is of no great help since it also avoids an exploration of what is an interactive problem.

Knowing that your attitudes and behaviour (professional and personal, verbal and non-verbal) influence the degree of difficulty of the interaction with a client can be useful. This knowledge, however, does not provide you with insight into the nature of the problem nor inform you how and why it has occurred nor guide your management of the counselling. Deciding how best to respond is often difficult, especially when you may be feeling exasperated by the non-compliant behaviour of your client.

Peter was a probation officer and an experienced counsellor who usually made brief written notes at the initial assessment interview. Peter believed that the reason his clients rarely commented on this practice was because he always asked them at the beginning if they had any objections. A particular young man, with whom Peter was working on aspects of his explosive temper, had not refused Peter's request and had begun to talk about his associated feelings of jealousy. He believed that his partner had been unfaithful to him and his mistrust had led him frequently to lose his temper and occasionally to become violent. He had served a prison sentence in relation to his violence and had recently been released back into the community.

When Peter interrupted to ask for evidence of the partner's infidelity, his client clammed up. Peter attempted to explore the reasons for this unexpected reaction with little success. The client then started to verbally abuse Peter, swearing and gesticulating menacingly and saying that he would continue the interview only if he could sit beside Peter, so he could see what was being written. Feeling emotionally bruised, Peter acquiesced but it was a quarter of an hour before he regained his usual professional composure.

In this and the next chapter we shall provide you with some ideas and concepts which may be of help in your professional encounters, by serving as a framework for analysing the nature and origins of complicated counselling transactions (such as that encountered with Sheila or by Peter). At best these will function as a rough guide but in the problematic and poorly charted territory into which you inevitably venture with clients you find 'difficult', even a crude map is better than none at all.

Counselling transactions

We use the term *counselling transaction* to refer to the interactive work which occurs between you and your client. In such transactions the two of you negotiate from different starting positions. Your clients contribute valuable knowledge about themselves and their affairs, while your expertise can clarify their difficulties. The term 'counselling transaction' de-emphasizes a view of the counsellor as sole expert and the client as merely the passive recipient of therapy.

Without an interactive approach the clients become the only object of study and hence the source of any difficulties in the counselling. Using the counselling transaction approach, by contrast, difficulties are located within the interaction. Ideally, therefore, you collaborate with your clients on their presenting problem or negotiate an alternative therapeutic agenda to address additional problems and conscientiously work towards a resolution.

Malcolm was a physically robust and tough-looking young man who initially complained of frequent nightmares. As these involved frightening and extreme violence (often involving mutilated babies and children) he would try to avoid sleep by taking illicit, stimulant drugs or else drink alcohol until he became unconscious. During discussion it emerged that Malcolm was also easily provoked into losing his temper. Malcolm and his counsellor agreed to work on this additional problem of how to manage his anger, partly because of the counsellor's concern for Malcolm's unborn child. (The counsellor had interviewed Malcolm's partner who, being six months pregnant, appeared concerned about Malcolm's problems and seemed to support his attempts to get help.)

Malcolm kept a diary of his nightmares to see whether the problem was resolving. After a week he stopped this. Over the next few weekly sessions Malcolm offered his counsellor a range of excuses for his lack of compliance with diary-keeping. In the meantime, he spent increasing amounts of his session time providing graphic details of his nightmares. These accounts were augmented by his reports of violent daytime thoughts which he recounted with apparent enthusiasm. The counsellor felt that Malcolm's repetitive presentation of this violent material kept him emotionally distant from her. Gradually, she noticed herself feeling increasingly anxious, while Malcolm seemed to be more relaxed. He appeared increasingly self-confident, even though he complained he was receiving no benefit from the sessions.

Malcolm's counsellor felt so concerned by her own rising anxiety, which she felt both during and between the sessions with Malcolm, that she discussed the situation in supervision with a senior colleague. It was then she realized that the original and negotiated focus of the counselling transaction had been lost. In discussing how to proceed, she and her supervisor decided that she should tell Malcolm that the focus of their work had been lost and agree with his view that no real progress had been made in achieving the originally negotiated goals. The daytime violent thoughts would be regarded as a problem which would acquire the status of an additional therapeutic goal. Since the power and extent of Malcolm's violent thoughts had been amply demonstrated, the counsellor would tell him to resume keeping the diary as, without this, the progress of the counselling transaction could not be adequately monitored.

Initially, Malcolm's counsellor had thought that the transaction was proceeding straightforwardly since Malcolm talked easily and attended regularly and punctually. It was only later that she realized that something more complicated was occurring. In particular, she noted that they had lost sight of the originally negotiated therapeutic goals. The counselling sessions were being hijacked by Malcolm's covert wish to avoid the psychic pain associated with a probing exploration of the origins of his problems. He increasingly dominated the transaction by filling the available time with repeated presentations of his problem which communicated no new factual information.

Whether difficulties are immediate and obvious, as with Sheila, or subtle and develop insidiously, as with Malcolm, you will urgently require a framework to characterize how the transaction has become complicated. Understanding the origins and mechanisms of the complication helps you to develop a more sophisticated overview of the particular transaction and can inform your subsequent therapeutic management.

Straightforward or complicated transactions

There are two types of counselling transaction, *straightforward* and *complicated* (see Norton and Smith, 1994). A straightforward counselling transaction is an *appropriately negotiated goal-oriented interaction, comprising public (including professional) and personal level components, which fulfils certain criteria* (see

Table 1.1 *Criteria for a straightforward clinical transaction*

The client is required to:
1 present a relevant complaint or problem;
2 own an appropriate degree of responsibility for the problem;
3 realistically want to be free of the problem;
4 based on sufficient trust and respect in the counsellor, disclose relevant information concerning the origin or perpetuation of the problem;
5 retain realistic expectations of counselling;
6 withstand the implicit demands and frustrations of counselling, including the effects of its termination.

As counsellor, you are required to:
7 make an initial assessment of the client's complaints or problems;
8 negotiate and pursue therapeutic goals with the client;
9 advise about the duration of counselling and any expected obstacles;
10 monitor your own reactions, including your emotional disposition towards the client, both within and between counselling sessions;
11 recognize when the client's expectations are unrealistic;
12 recognize when your own limits are reached;
13 recognize when the client's behaviour indicates risk of danger to anybody;
14 manage the termination of the counselling transaction and consider the need for other psychological interventions.

Table 1.1). In a straightforward counselling transaction you negotiate therapeutic goals and agree a means to achieve them, allowing for the interruption caused by the usual resistances, frustrations and distractions. You both pursue these goals conscientiously. You continue to a mutually agreed termination or, in the case of counselling the dying client or when offering long-term supportive counselling, agree not to terminate.

A complicated counselling transaction, by contrast, is one in which there is a *significant, non-transient departure(s) from the straightforward counselling transaction at the public or personal interaction level or both*. The criteria listed in Table 1.1 can be used to identify factors which characterize the particular complicated counselling transaction. Thus, for example, Malcolm presented a relevant complaint, namely his 'nightmares' and difficulty with his anger, thus fulfilling criterion (1). Subsequently, however, he failed to own an appropriate degree of responsibility for his complaint, not fulfilling criterion (2) and did not appear to want to be rid of it, that is not fulfilling criterion (3). His counsellor utilized her skills in monitoring her personal reaction to him, fulfilling criterion (10) but identified this as being a departure from how she usually felt in her professional encounters. This particular counselling transaction is thus characterized by departures from the straightforward transaction at criteria (2) and (3).

Complicating factors may arise in a hitherto straightforward transaction or else be present as such from the start. Nevertheless, complicated transactions can, at least in some instances, be converted to the straightforward. Often this requires 'personal' aspects of the transaction becoming a negotiated 'public' therapeutic goal or being taken into account to re-direct the public level interaction, as with Malcolm. Sometimes, the personal aspect is raised on to the public agenda but only to state that it is not an appropriate therapeutic goal. In such ways, the public level counselling activity is reinforced by educating the client about what is and what is not a realistic therapeutic goal and mutual disappointment is minimized (see also Chapters 6 and 7).

Public and personal interaction levels

Your counselling transaction can be viewed as comprising two parallel and inter-dependent relationships. One of these is essentially public, in the sense of being accessible to the usual methods of professional scrutiny and of being shaped by society's expectations of your professional role and the complementary role of your client. The other relationship is much more personal and is relatively hidden. The public level interaction of the transaction is dependent upon the support of some, for example an appropriate level of mutual trust and respect, but not other potential aspects of the personal level interaction, for example erotic attraction or an intimate sexual relationship.

Some of the evidence of departures from the criteria necessary for a straightforward counselling transaction is readily observable, since it involves gross behavioural departures at the public or personal level, such as Sheila's failure to enter the consulting room or Peter's client's angry tirade. Other evidence may be subtler and consequently more difficult to recognize, such as the rising level of anxiety which Malcolm's counsellor felt. She was unsure of the origin of the anxiety since it derived, in part at least, from her personal reaction to her client's intonation and facial expression.

Public and personal level departures from the criteria for a straightforward counselling transaction can be organized to form a transaction 'window' through which to view your counselling

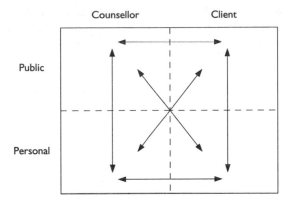

Figure 1.1 *Transaction window: public–personal, counsellor–client interaction*

transaction. These aspects inevitably influence one another in a complex way (see Figure 1.1). As a result of this set of inter-relationships, a change in one level or in one participant can lead to a change at another level or in the other participant. Much counselling work involves the facilitation of your client to disclose personal information at the public level in order to elucidate the presenting problem. You achieve this by influencing your client through your public level activity, for example using suitable questions or prompts and via your personal level attributes, including empathy, genuineness and non-possessive warmth (Truax et al., 1966). (See also Chapters 2 and 4 for a more detailed discussion.)

You and your client have different expectations of one another. If these are unrealistic or are not made explicit, then tensions may result which, if not resolved, can complicate the counselling transaction by straining and distorting your interaction. The following vignette exemplifies this point.

*Andrew was in his mid-forties and successful in his pro-
fessional life. His children were nearing the end of their
formal education and he and his wife had been looking
forward to spending more time together. However, the
country's economic climate changed for the worse and
Andrew's international business required him to move his
work location and to work longer hours. This necessitated*

renting accommodation close to the new business office, being away from his family more and spending more time with his personal assistant, with whom he started a sexual relationship.

Andrew became anxious and depressed and increased his intake of alcohol and tobacco, which exacerbated a long-standing respiratory condition. His GP, whom he consulted about his chest complaint, diagnosed a 'mixed affective state' (based on the presence of both anxiety and depressive symptoms) and referred him to a counsellor.

Andrew impressed his counsellor with his alert mind, which was retained in spite of his anxiety and depression. Initially, the 'halo' effect of Andrew's intelligence meant that his counsellor expected Andrew to have insight into his psychological problems. In fact, Andrew was not aware that in his complex circumstances (he did not want to upset his family but nor did he want to lose the excitement of his relationship with his personal assistant) it would be difficult for him to stop feeling anxious and depressed. Both at work and at home Andrew had been used to solving problems quickly, through delegating responsibility to others and being unquestioningly obeyed. He expected, inappropriately, that his counsellor could be left to sort out a solution to the problems and, in effect, report back to Andrew on a job well done!

Much of your own particular professional style and many of your general communication and therapeutic skills will have been learned without obvious or conscious effort, as many of them are also the skills of your ordinary, non-professional life. Other skills will have been acquired more deliberately and at a considerable personal, possibly financial, cost. However, even if much of the counselling work proceeds without you having a sense of conscious strain and without undue deliberation, this neither diminishes the complexity of the intrinsic therapeutic task nor the accomplishment inherent in achieving a successful therapeutic outcome. In Andrew's case an early task for his counsellor was to engage him meaningfully as a client who was active within the counselling process. This included helping him to realize that there was not a simple, quick or pain-free solution to his problems.

The public level of the interaction between you and your client is shaped and confined by pressure to conform to the social roles which are ascribed to both of you by the society in which you live (Turner, 1962). Your role as counsellor may include many elements, making it difficult to perform. You may be expected to be something of a friend, parent, priest, psychoanalyst and policeman! The role is not without its limits, however, and you will probably recognize what it feels like to be pushed to, or beyond, these. When you feel that more is expected or demanded of you than you can, or perhaps should, provide, you may label your client as 'difficult'. A knowledge of the constraints put on your counselling transactions by the culture and society in which you work can therefore form a useful orientation to help you negotiate overt, appropriate limits and help you maintain these in your public level interaction with clients.

The vast majority of counselling transactions do not require you to deviate from the counsellor role prescribed by society. Thus, you approach most clients, even those you do not feel a particular affinity towards, with an attitude which is *usual for you* and is part of your professional style, even though you may have only an incomplete knowledge of its constituents. So long as the therapeutic work progresses, with negotiated goals being achieved as expected, you may have no reason to question your usual style and method of relating to your clients.

Even though working towards an agreed outcome may involve experiencing painful emotional states, you will probably consider these a relevant part of the therapeutic work. For example, the anger and sadness, which both you and your client may experience in bereavement counselling, may be emotionally uncomfortable but is relevant to the goals of the transaction and does not affect the overall quality and process of your counselling transaction. You are able to retain your usual capacity for empathy and insight and you deploy your therapeutic skills so that your observations or suggestions are both intellectually and emotionally accessible to your client. In this situation even the strains of ending the transaction are borne well enough to permit a termination which is not itself traumatizing.

The apparently straightforward therapeutic work which you conduct with most of your clients, most of the time, is the result of a collaborative effort which is a considerable psychological achievement. You forge a contract to work together to achieve particular goals even when your respective starting positions, in terms of expectations and motivation, are different. The smooth process of your straightforward counselling transaction may mask the considerable emotional and intellectual effort which is entailed.

If you mainly deploy your skills intuitively you may have difficulty in resolving interpersonal problems arising with your clients, since acknowledging these problems may induce pain, frustration and guilt, which impair your capacity to think creatively. Struggling intellectually as well as experientially, with uncomfortable emotions, however, is an important part of the process of therapeutic work. As far as possible you undertake the two tasks in parallel.

Ideally, your capacity to think does not sink when you experience a tide of strong emotions. When, however, you encounter thoughts, feelings or exhibit behaviour towards your clients which are outside your usual range, your usual rationality and clarity of thought may be impaired. The presence of disturbance in your usual professional disposition or departures from your professional composure (personal level activity) should impress you as being of potential therapeutic significance and lead you to consider the reasons for them. If you cannot think during the session then you may be able to outside, either in supervision or during your 'free' time (see Chapters 4 and 7).

The role and the person

Barbara, a social worker who was undertaking an intensive psychodynamic training felt embarrassed in supervision that she could recall very little detail from her recent sessions with a female client. This young woman, who had been physically and sexually abused by family members for much of her childhood and adolescence, had presented with difficulties acknowledging that she was gay.

Barbara had noted a pattern in her client's relationships where she became attracted to psychologically vulnerable, younger women. The relationship would start platonically. However, once the younger partner demonstrated any increased self-confidence or attempted to assert her independence, Barbara's client would become extremely angry. Her rage was only relieved by violent sex, including partially asphyxiating the other woman, almost to the point of unconsciousness.

Barbara was aware of her client's extremely poor relationship with her father (one of the men who had sexually abused her) but, when she asked her about her mother's role in the family, her client immediately fell silent. She then began to speak increasingly quickly and loudly about both her intense mistrust of women in general and how misunderstood she felt by Barbara.

In the ensuing sessions her anger did not subside and almost every direct question Barbara asked provoked another tirade. During supervision, Barbara realized that she had been fearful that her client would attack her and that consequently she had become more interrogatory, an approach which increased her client's defensive anger. Only after a further eighteen months of therapy could her client reveal some of her deep-seated sense of despair at having been let down by her mother, whom she felt should have protected her from the sexual advances of both her father and her abusing uncles.

Your capacity to give and your client's capacity to receive care form an important part of the personal level interaction. Caring may involve tolerating negative or ambivalent feelings either because they are part of your personal level interaction, such as Barbara's fear, or because your attempts to care are not gratefully received. For you it may feel as if your 'care' is thrown back in your face; for your clients, receiving care may rekindle feelings of inferiority, humiliation and extreme vulnerability. They have often regarded feelings of neediness as weaknesses, which they have striven to avoid or hide. Heeding any advice you might offer may require effort and involve frustration and psychic pain, especially if it requires significant lifestyle changes, for example giving up an addiction to alcohol or drugs or, as with Barbara's client, stopping violent behaviour.

Barbara temporarily lost her usual capacity to remember clearly and think about her personal reaction to her client. She was initially unaware of her fear of being attacked and, as she did not register feeling this emotion, she remained unaware of her public level departure from her normal style to a more interrogatory one. What she had noticed was that she could not recall much of the factual content of the counselling sessions.

Your personal need to provide care or give support and your clients' inability to receive help or their capacity to render it useless are moulded by your early familial and later social relationships.

These relationships, which involve care-giving and care-receiving, act as a model for all your subsequent relationships or transactions which incorporate 'care' (see Chapter 2). In particular, your relationship with parents or parent substitutes, during the early years when identity and personality are formed, is crucial. As a professional carer, the more you become aware of the less obvious motives for your choice of career, the less likely is it that frustrations in personal level interactions will impact adversely on public level ones and vice versa, potentially complicating the counselling transaction through your having become over-zealous (Searles, 1979).

Problems in performing the social role of therapist or of client (and in understanding and respecting the other party's reciprocal role) may result in departures at the personal level. For example, some clients may believe that you have limitless time, patience and therapeutic resources at your disposal and act accordingly. They appear to ignore that you are involved in a professional relationship with them and only have finite professional and personal resources. It is as if they wish to avoid the psychological distress they would experience if they thought of you as both a person and a professional. Thus, they are unable to see you as somebody who has limits but who, nevertheless, is willing to work up to these to help them.

While some clients act as if they expect limitless help, others perceive you as actively withholding help. They behave as if they see you only in a professional role, devoid of any personal attributes. This perspective often derives from their past negative experiences with authority figures who have had little respect for their needs or feelings and provided only minimal care or abused their power. The possibility of you being a willing and helpful counsellor either does not enter their minds or, if it does, then only fleetingly. They fail to see their counsellor as a person and may relate to you as if you were more machine than human being.

As counsellor you too are subject to pressures and stresses which distort your perception of your clients. Frustrating situations can lead you to lose sight of your clients as people with whom you are in a professional relationship and who may have little capacity to fulfil the demands of the client role. This predominantly personal view can result in you holding your clients responsible for, if not being guilty of, their presenting problems. Rather than helping them to fulfil their role as client more completely, you act as if you are content for them to take a quite different role, that of the 'difficult client'. Although this allows you to withdraw personally, it means that at least some of the time you avoid carrying out your professional responsibility to your clients. Ideally, therefore, you should retain a capacity to differentiate between clients as people and their unwillingness, or else their inability, to perform their appropriate role as clients. In practice this is easier said than done.

> *Helen was quickly in tears during her first meeting with her counsellor. She only slowly recovered her composure and, with sensitive questioning, the counsellor attempted to complete an initial assessment. He had formulated Helen's presenting problem, self-mutilation, as stemming from low self-esteem. He felt that the session might have broken down completely had it not been for his insight into her distress and the emotional support he provided. The latter had taken much of the inter-view time and, as a result, his assessment was much less comprehensive than usual. Thus his formulation, although accurate up to a point, was based on incomplete information. At the time, however, he considered it to be sufficient.*
>
> *For the next four months, the counsellor felt that Helen was progressing, since he took her continuous weeping during the sessions as evidence that important psychological work was underway. He began to look forward to the sessions with her, despite the fact that she revealed no further personal material and spent most of the time sobbing. Feeling such misplaced pride in the 'progress' Helen was making, he was completely taken aback when, without tears but with considerable anger, she declared that she would be terminating her counselling since, although she recognized the genuineness of his attempts to help her, she felt that nothing had changed. The counsellor felt devastated and asked his client to prove that she had not changed. Helen had little difficulty in listing many more problems than her deliberate self-harm. At the end of the session the counsellor was left not knowing whether Helen would return.*

The counsellor felt he had been lulled into a false sense of professional well-being. Noting this reaction sooner, he might have considered the need to strengthen Helen's ability to fulfil her client's role.

Summary

It is important to avoid stigmatizing certain of your clients by labelling them as 'difficult', since this neither furthers your understanding of how the 'difficulty' arose nor indicates how you should best respond. Instead, the stigmatic label taints the 'whole person' of your clients and, as a result, you no longer see them as a sum of many parts but view them within the context of the label, seeing less than the whole person.

Your therapeutic difficulty is intrinsically interactive, since both you and your clients, to some extent, play a part in its genesis. An awareness of the interactive nature of the cause of these difficulties can guide you towards its solution. You must first, however, recognize the signs, especially the early ones, of potentially significant departures in the interaction so that, with appropriate intervention, these departures from the straightforward transaction do not progress to become entrenched and result in a complicated counselling transaction.

The term counselling transaction incorporates the two levels of your interaction, public and personal. These can only be artificially differentiated. Considering them separately, however, reveals the complexity of the professional encounter and facilitates an understanding of how easily its smooth progress and successful outcome is susceptible to a variety of complicating influences. These can arise in either the public or personal level interactions between you and your client.

Significant departures from the criteria of the straightforward counselling transaction can arise when you and your clients do not or cannot differentiate between the person and their role. The result is that the person and the role become either conflated or dislocated. For your clients, this leads to unrealistic expectations of yourself and of therapy. These can be set too high, too low or sometimes oscillating between the two. For you, the clients simply become 'difficult' and can be rationalized to be out of the reach of your professional help. You may give up trying to understand the incapacity or obstacle your clients have to taking their role appropriately. When there is a breakdown in the capacity to differentiate between the person and the role, by either participant, the success of the whole counselling transaction is jeopardized, because of a complicating interactive effect which can hold both you and your client in its grip, sometimes irreversibly.

2

The Influence of Past Interactions

Your clients' early experiences of being cared for shape their expectations of and behaviour in their intimate relationships and their relationships with professional carers, such as yourself. Especially if these early experiences have been chronically unsatisfactory, your clients' attitudes and behaviour in asking for help may be maladaptive and compounded by any difficulties you have with responding to others' demands and offering help. If these difficulties resonate, even small departures from the straightforward counselling transaction can become amplified. Your clients' expectations of you and yours of them, both of which have been coloured by past experiences of being cared for and providing care, may be incompatible with the effective pursuit of public level therapeutic goals. Indeed, personal level goals may successfully compete against the overt goals of the overall transaction.

Sometimes your clients' difficulty in receiving help is as obvious as that of Sheila, who was unable to enter her counsellor's consulting room (page 1). At other times their difficulties may present subtly, like Helen's tears which 'compelled' her therapist to jettison some of his public level assessment tasks. In these circumstances it is as if an interpersonal goal is tacitly agreed between the two of you, which can supplant public level goals. Such departures from the straightforward may be difficult to detect, especially if either one of you experiences them positively, as did Helen's counsellor. Where consistent emotional, physical or sexual abuse and neglect has occurred in either or both of your own and your clients' early life, there is an increased risk of an impaired ability later on to distinguish between the person and their professional role (see

Chapter 1). This inability includes a difficulty in differentiating between aspects of present and past interactions involving the giving and receiving of care. As a consequence, the therapeutic relationship can be distorted so that inappropriate expectations or demands can be made or met by either person, without question. In such a distorted 'therapeutic' relationship, specific patterns of interaction may become established which complicate your clinical transactions. In this chapter we discuss how past interactions can affect, in the present, both the reciprocal role-taking and the overall pattern of public and personal interaction within the counselling transaction.

Past interactions and current role-taking

Early attachments and later expectations
All human beings display a need to form strong emotional attachments to others. This need is present from the beginning of life and continues as part of normal childhood and adult behaviour (Weiss, 1991). Young children develop expectations about themselves and their attachment figures based on the style and quality of parental or other primary care-givers' interactions with them (Bowlby, 1973). These expectations greatly influence the nature of the child's future attachments and development by either enhancing or diminishing their capacity for healthy emotional, cognitive and social development (Ainsworth, 1991).

Children who have no basic trust in the reliability and appropriate responsiveness of their care-givers are less likely to become securely attached to them, remaining fearful of separation and lacking in confidence and trust. Carried into adulthood, their earlier patterns profoundly affect their later capacity to both give and receive help or care. This has implications for the counsellor–client relationship, as was clearly demonstrated by Sheila and her counsellor's interaction.

> *Sheila, who had found it difficult to enter the consulting room, was the elder of two siblings. Her mother was super-ficially a timid woman who had been shielded from the full force of her own parents' stormy relationship and violent tempers by her attachment to her older sister who, in effect, had mothered her. Sheila's mother had married early, partly to escape her frightening family life and partly because she*

fell in love with a violent young man whom she viewed as strong enough to face up to her father.

Sheila's parents' marriage broke down when Sheila was six. Two months later her father committed suicide. Her mother never completely recovered from this loss and began a longing search for a replacement partner, which involved a series of unsatisfactory, brief relationships with men who were either aggressive and dominated her or who allowed her to mother them in an infantilizing manner. As a result, Sheila's childhood was characterized by multiple attachments, separations and losses and she coped emotionally, perhaps like her aunt, by obtaining vicarious care through looking after a younger sibling. Like her own mother, Sheila left home early to marry but this relationship failed and she returned home. When her younger brother left home to take up a new job, Sheila's eating disorder began. Her brother returned home out of concern for Sheila and persuaded her to have counselling.

Sheila was reluctant to accept the idea of counselling as she felt that if she were to sincerely request help she would be exposed to feeling vulnerable. For Sheila, counselling represented unfamiliar emotional territory and her expectations of it, especially the requirement to reveal personal aspects of herself, filled her with horror and revulsion. She could only imagine that the counselling relationship would be a repetition of her earlier attachments which, in her mind, were associated inevitably with her inner needs remaining unmet, a premature loss of the relationship and a consequent resurgence of ambivalent feelings.

Distinguishing between professional and personal care

At the time of their first interview, Helen's counsellor was feeling uncharacteristically low as his mother had gone into hospital a few days previously. A single parent, his mother had suffered post-natal depression following her son's birth and had continued to suffer from bouts of depression throughout his childhood and adolescence. As an adult, Helen's counsellor was sensitized by his early experiences to respond to his client's tears as if they had to be dried post-haste. It was as if he were transported back in time when, not understanding the actual causes of his mother's depression, he felt inappropriately responsible both for having caused and for having to repair what he perceived as the damage done to her. He felt that he had partially accomplished this task with respect to his mother and the resulting increase in his self-esteem bolstered his belief that he was especially talented in dealing with the needs of depressed people and influenced his career choice.

Helen was allowing her counsellor to feel fulfilled at the expense of getting her own emotional needs met through being able to present her problems clearly. Her counsellor convinced himself that depriving himself of one of his public level goals, in deciding not to make a detailed assessment, was in his client's interests. His failure to identify the departures from the straightforward performing of client and counsellor roles meant that he did not distinguish appropriately between the public and personal level requirements of the counselling transaction. Even if such departures as his do not require urgent attention or immediate rectification, their early recognition is important if significant departures are to be avoided.

Obstacles to seeking and receiving care

Many clients find that directly asking for help is humiliating. They believe that the fact that they need help is proof of their inadequacy and failure as a person. They feel transported back to a time when any expression of need was met with inconsistent or other unsatisfactory responses. In their past, attempts to obtain appropriate care may have been met with derision or anger, or have been ignored, or relegated in importance or else have been totally replaced by, those of their carer. The legacy of these past styles of 'caring' is that your clients may have frightening, inappropriately high or low, or else contradictory expectations of the counselling transaction.

Understandably, your clients may be ambivalent about your ability to respond maturely and appropriately to them as their counsellor. As adults, your clients have intellectual knowledge of the social responsibility implicit in your professional role and expect you to fulfil your public level duties in this respect. Their previous repeated experiences of being let down by those in authority, however, mean that they anticipate and sadly sometimes receive an unsatisfactory response.

Helen's counsellor's over-zealous comforting of her left Helen playing a relatively passive role. This meant that some important aspects of the ordinary 'sick role' behaviour, such as adequately presenting her problems and providing relevant personal information relating to her past, were not expected of her. This lowered public level expectation reinforced Helen's pre-existing feelings of worthlessness in her current interaction with her counsellor. The result was an inadequate assessment and a client who felt frustrated and humiliated. The assessment process became merged with the start of counselling proper and each new session became a repeat of the previous one, with no genuine therapeutic alliance being established. Helen's history was repeating itself, she felt that her strengths were unrecognized and her difficulties unaddressed. She felt unvalued by her counsellor, feelings she had had previously in relation to her late father.

Obstacles to providing care

When facets of your personal history resonate with aspects of your clients' histories, as with Helen's counsellor, it can be difficult to assess the appropriateness of your clients' presented problems and whether you have the ability to deal with them. This is because you do not move as smoothly and effectively as usual between your public and personal levels, accurately monitoring and maintaining each of them. You thereby lose some of your capacity to evaluate your clients and to monitor the professional relationship.

Sometimes, your capacities are diminished by the strength of an emotional tide which disturbs your usual public–personal equilibrium, allowing the personal to swamp or undermine the public level agenda. For a time at least, you lose your ability to distinguish between your public role responsibilities and your personal wishes. Alternatively, you divorce yourself from the natural human feelings which arise when you are in contact with a person who needs your help and lose contact with your usual emotional sensitivity and reactivity. Your public–personal equilibrium is thereby upset, with the public level dominating the personal level.

Even if you have a thorough knowledge of and good ability to think about your interpersonal relationships, you will not be able to maintain a balanced and objective stance all the time, with all your clients. Indeed, it might be argued that much of what is therapeutic reflects your clients sensing that you are human and, like them, having to struggle to understand the confusing world of emotions and relationships. Inevitably, you will form a better rapport with some clients than others and, as a consequence, be better able to help them. With these clients you have succeeded in integrating aspects of your public and personal roles and will have been able to avoid the extremes of either emotional over-involvement or unhelpful detachment.

Past and current interaction patterns

When previous interactions have habitually frustrated your clients' need for care, it is likely that current interactions, which involve the asking for and receiving of care, will be infiltrated by or suffused with aspects of the original relationships. As a result, the whole counselling transaction can become distorted simultaneously at both its public and personal levels. This distortion can be conceptualized as arising when the usual equilibrium between the public and personal level interactions of the straightforward counselling transaction has shifted significantly.

Ideally, the public–personal equilibrium allows for an adequate expression of those personal aspects which can beneficially infuse and inform the public level interaction – sufficient warmth, trust and respect. The blending of your own and your clients' individual personalities, which enrich the counselling transaction, is facilitated. A pronounced shift of the public–personal equilibrium, however, results in the possibility that inappropriate personal aspects dominate or that appropriate personal aspects are partially excluded or absent. As a result of either shift, the transaction is at risk of becoming complicated.

Evidence of an equilibrium shift in the direction of personal level dominance may be seen in your clients' exaggerated requests for help. The content, as well as the mode of expression of your clients' requests, may be beyond conventionally acceptable limits. Peter's client, for example, having erupted in anger, insisted on sitting beside Peter which meant that Peter no longer had easy eye contact with his client nor his usual amount of personal space. This particular client's upbringing had been marked by multiple separations from his parents during his mother's admissions to a psychiatric hospital for treatment of her schizophrenic illness. As a result, he was frequently placed in temporary foster care, which provided him with widely ranging standards of care and left him with little expectation that Peter would respond appropriately to his requests for help. Thus Peter could understand some of the reasons for his client's personal level domination.

An equilibrium shift in the direction of public level dominance may be reflected in your clients' demeanour when, as a consequence, their requests for help convey an impersonal or unemotional quality, suggesting a lack of authenticity and sincerity. This understated style of presentation could lead you either to dismiss their problems as trivial or to regard your clients as phoney or superficial. Malcolm's repetition of his violent thoughts had the effect of infuriating and, later, emotionally numbing his counsellor. She did not take them as seriously as, later, she thought she should have.

If you are alert to the ways in which shifts in the public–personal equilibrium can manifest themselves within the counselling transaction, you may avoid the automatic responses to your clients which maintain the re-enactment of aspects of past styles of relating. Without such an awareness, your own and your clients' unhelpful responses may compound one another and produce a stalemate. The attraction of such an interaction is that it is 'familiar' to both you and your clients, but, since it is dictated by your respective past interactions or previously failed professional encounters, it often runs counter to the straightforward pursuit of the current therapeutic goals. Peter's interaction with his client and Malcolm's with his counsellor were re-enactments of earlier interactions dominated by power and control rather than by mutual trust and respect.

Transaction windows
Shifts in the public–personal equilibrium of the counselling transaction can be represented diagrammatically through the use of the *transaction window* (page 7). Figure 2.1 represents a shifted equilibrium in the direction of public level dominance, and Figure 2.2 a shift in the direction of personal dominance.

The balance of the public–personal equilibrium within the overall counselling transaction is influenced by factors deriving from both you and your clients. The initial shift or change may arise in either of you. It is more important to notice the fact of any equilibrium shift, however, than to determine its origin. Helen's counsellor needed to notice, therefore, his heightened emotional responsiveness to Helen and his more active comforting of his client, following her tearfulness, as evidence of his own public–personal equilibrium shift. Specifically, he should have noticed, possibly with the aid of supervision, that he had assumed a more

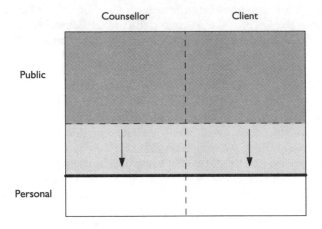

Figure 2.1 *Diagrammatic representation of public level dominance*

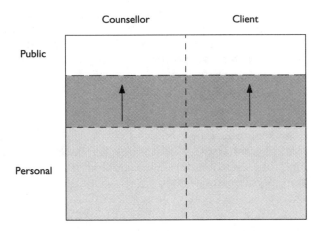

Figure 2.2 *Diagrammatic representation of personal level dominance*

unthinking and emotionally intense style of relating to Helen than was usual, even for himself. Alternatively, he might have registered signs of departure from the pursuit of the public level goals of the transaction. This overall style of interacting was 'familiar' to him since it represented a re-living of important elements of his own past relationship with his mother (page 17). Using the transaction window, the resultant, relatively static, therapeutic situation between Helen and her counsellor, can be represented diagrammatically (in Figure 2.3). This figure illustrates a complicated counselling transaction where a significant, non-transient departure from the counsellor's notional straightforward transaction has become firmly established.

Initially, you will not know about the precise nature and style of your clients' previous interactions and you are therefore at a disadvantage when you need to identify when they are being re-lived or re-enacted in the current transaction. Although you may lack evidence that enables you to identify and describe your clients' overall styles, you may be able to recognize individual facets or departures from the straightforward counselling transaction (see page 5), which provide you with important information about your clients' past and current styles of relating. Developing an awareness of the constituents of your own professional style, in terms of your habitual responses to specific aspects of your clients' histories and problems, aids you in this task. The manner in which you depart from your usual professional style may offer clues about your clients' styles of relating to you. Indeed such clues, which often reflect important aspects of past interactions, can be used to formulate hypotheses about the nature of these interactions and are especially useful when your clients do not talk about their pasts spontaneously or when you are attempting to return the transaction to the straightforward (see Chapter 7).

'Ordinary' clients and the counsellor's professional style
Your own professional style, comprising public and personal level constituents, includes the notion of yourself in relation to an 'ordinary' client, within a straightforward counselling transaction. Using the transaction window, its territory and limits can be represented diagrammatically (in Figure 2.4). Counselling transactions which stray outside your usual range are at an increased risk of becoming complicated, because of the degree of public–personal disequilibrium within the counselling transaction at that time.

Shifts in the public–personal equilibrium can be depicted diagrammatically by vertical movement of the horizontal axis. A significant equilibrium shift in the direction of public dominance is denoted by a continuous solid line as in Figure 2.1 and a significant

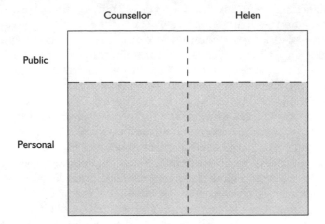

Figure 2.3 *Diagrammatic representation of the complicated clinical transaction between Helen and her counsellor*

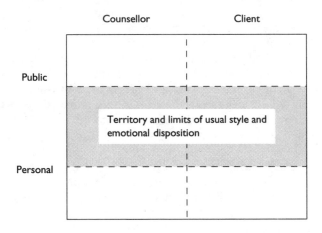

Figure 2.4 *Diagram showing limits of non-significant shifts in the public–personal equilibrium*

shift in the opposite direction by a dashed line as in Figure 2.2. Significant shifts in the equilibrium mean that the straightforward clinical transaction is at serious risk of becoming complicated unless these changes are only transient. This is because the new equilibrium is less sensitively poised since it is maintained either by strong personal level aspects or by the virtual absence of any personal level involvement. The resulting patterns of interaction can be very stable and difficult to dismantle. The longer they persist the harder they are to influence. When finally there is movement, this can be dramatic as with Helen's announcement of her decision to terminate her therapy abruptly.

Basic interaction patterns

Certain patterns of interaction within the counselling transaction are particularly stable because they reflect a significant disequilibrium, either towards public or personal dominance. However, evidence of the patterns may be difficult to detect because the very stability of the resultant interaction masks the complicated status, by suggesting a straightforward character to the transaction. The transaction thus may appear to be straightforward when it is not. Some basic interaction patterns can, however, be recognized by their distinctive, albeit subtle, signs. These signs may show in you or your clients.

You and your client can be involved in: (1) a mechanical interchange, devoid of emotion – public dominance of the public–personal equilibrium; (2) an interaction where intense and sometimes primitive feelings, thoughts and behaviour predominate – personal dominance; or (3) enacting complementary positions with respect to one another, that is one party is dominated by the public level, with little personal level component, while the other is almost entirely dominated by the personal level – mixed dominance (see Figure 2.5).

The diagrams in Figure 2.5 represent three basic interaction patterns, the recognition of which may help you clarify styles of interaction in your counselling work. Most counsellors will have a particular experience of public dominance, although this will vary between transactions and according to whether their clients are in a complementary or, alternatively, an equivalent position. Experiences where the public level functioning is flooded by the personal level will also have a distinctive flavour which varies from transaction to transaction according to the predominant emotions engendered. The emotional climate of your own early formative interactions influences how you experience and process these emotions. You will see some as positive, some as negative. In

1 Public dominance

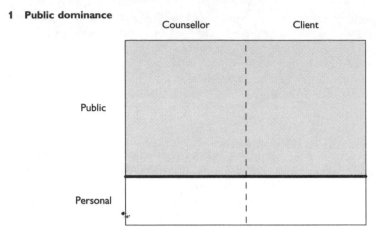

2 Personal dominance

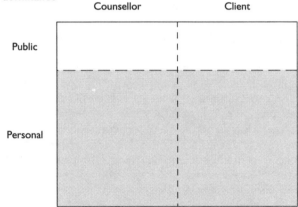

Figure 2.5 *Basic interaction patterns*

either case, as your earlier experiences have familiarized you with
a particular constellation of emotions, it may be difficult for you to
identify personal dominance as a departure from the straightforward counselling transaction.

1 Public dominance
This interactive pattern is characterized by a public–personal
disequilibrium in which public level aspects of both counsellor and

3 Mixed dominance

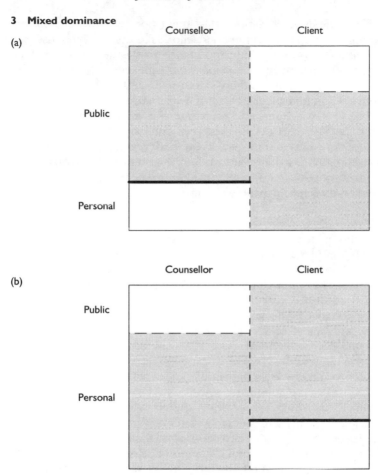

client dominate the counselling transaction. Andrew and his counsellor's transaction, for example, quickly became an emotionless, symptom-listing and advice-giving exercise. Andrew expected that he merely had to enumerate his complaints of anxiety and depression and that his counsellor would do the rest. As Andrew's counsellor imagined that his client was more resourceful and insightful than was really the case, he believed that allowing Andrew to articulate his depressive thoughts and providing some advice about anxiety management would suffice for counselling.

The therapeutic sterility of this interaction pattern may not be immediately apparent to the counsellor. Like Andrew's counsellor, you may fail to attach any importance to the fact that you feel emotionally dis-engaged in your client's presence. Typical of this pattern of interaction, Andrew's counsellor felt no qualms of conscience when he cancelled one of Andrew's sessions at very short notice. This was unusual behaviour and an unusual response, which he failed to consider as evidence of a public–personal equilibrium shift in himself. If he had been able to think in counselling transaction terms about the public and personal level interactions between himself and Andrew, he might not have mistaken their mechanical exchange for a meaningful interchange.

2   Personal dominance

With this pattern of interaction the shift in the public–personal equilibrium of the counselling transaction is in the direction of the personal level with respect to both parties. The personal level interaction between Helen and her counsellor, for example, very quickly swamped their public level work. Her counsellor relegated the importance of his conventional practice of making a thorough initial assessment of his client in favour of the short-term goal of relieving her overt distress. He felt compelled to be particularly active in the sessions, believing that without his ministrations some disaster would ensue. In the emotional grip of this situation, he was unable to pursue adequately the public level goals of the transaction.

Identifying such an interaction pattern may be problematic, since, as with Helen and her counsellor, there may be an illusion that therapeutic work is taking place because the true state of affairs has been masked by the prominence of overt emotion which may be viewed by counsellor or client as progress.

3   Mixed dominance

The third basic interaction pattern represents the enactment of a complementary style of interaction, where public level activity is dominant in one party and personal activity in the other. Like the first two interaction patterns, it can be stable. Its stability arises from the fact that it is based on the re-living of past interaction patterns which are largely or completely outside ordinary awareness. In the counselling transaction it reflects the simultaneous presence of disequilibrium in both counsellor and client but with each shifted in the opposite direction. It can be exemplified by two of the counselling transactions already referred to in Chapter 1, namely, that of Barbara and her client and Malcolm and his counsellor.

Barbara, the social worker and trainee psychotherapist, who became increasingly interrogatory in her interaction with her young physically and sexually abused client, was not aware of this change in her own behaviour, which reflected an increase in her public level activity and a concomitant decrease in her personal level responsiveness. In supervision, however, she saw the link between her fear of being attacked by her client (experienced more in-between than during sessions) and her public level behaviour of asking more questions, which left her little or no time to contemplate her fear. Barbara's client experienced her questions as an attack and reacted with defensive anger.

Barbara did not appreciate how disconnected she was emotionally. The impact of this on her client was the latter's diminished capacity to fulfil the role of client, since she felt overwhelmed by her own anger. Consequently, she was unable to tell her therapist how painfully she experienced being let down by her mother. Her anger was further fuelled by feelings in the present of being let down by Barbara, because of Barbara's failure to understand her predicament. Thus, the present interaction with Barbara echoed important aspects of her past interactions with her mother.

This failure of empathy consisted of two components. First, Barbara's fear and defensive reaction went undetected during the sessions so that she was working almost exclusively in her public level. Secondly, in the grip of intense emotions, her client had decreased access to a more mature capacity to communicate distress.

Malcolm and his counsellor enacted the above situation in reverse. Malcolm, in spite of his 'complaint' of violent fantasies, did not seem to exhibit or experience any emotional connection with his problems. His counsellor, although initially emotionally disconnected, felt increasingly uneasy and became a worried and helpless onlooker during the sessions. She felt impotent in the face of a client who ignored her contributions and whose constant complaining continued unabated. This echoed the past situation, when Malcolm had been the helpless onlooker of parental violence. The counsellor's usual state of public–personal equilibrium was only revived in her later discussion with a senior colleague.

In this interaction pattern Malcolm performed his public level, client's role but without conviction, which is evidence of public level dominance of his public–personal equilibrium. His counsellor, on the other hand, was unable to function at her usual public level, at least during the sessions, because she felt overwhelmed by her own personal emotional reaction.

Relationship between basic interaction patterns and complicated counselling transactions

The three basic interaction patterns are not synonymous with complicated counselling transactions since they may represent only transient departures from the straightforward. The longer such patterns continue unrecognized or unchallenged, however, the more likely they are to become established and lead to the transaction becoming complicated. As a result of this, the interaction patterns come to characterize certain complicated counselling transactions, even though their individual characteristics will vary between transactions. Within some transactions such interaction patterns can be detected almost from the start (for example, that of Helen) but in others they are only seen later (for example, with Malcolm).

The two sub-variants of the mixed dominance pattern can oscillate, often with little or no warning. The result is that the disequilibrium of each party suddenly shifts into its opposite. Stability is almost instantaneously regained. However, there remains the possibility of further dramatic shifts back in the original direction. A pattern of public dominance can also convert to that of personal dominance with equal speed and without obvious warning. A shift in the opposite direction, personal dominance to public, is also possible although less common. Shifts between public and personal dominance tend to have a slower timescale to their oscillation than those within the mixed dominance pattern. The effect of such abrupt transitions, from one basic interaction pattern to another, is to increase the likelihood that the counselling transaction becomes complicated.

Summary

Clients whose histories are marked by significant abuse or neglect may have a seriously impaired capacity to collaborate in both the negotiation and carrying out of the work required to achieve therapeutic goals. This is because of the re-activation, in the present interaction, of aspects of past, frustrating 'caring' relationships in which needs were habitually and variously unmet. The resulting inappropriate expectations of the counselling transaction may be obvious, when manifested by gross departures from the straightforward transaction, whether at the public or personal level. Sometimes, however, the departures are subtle but nonetheless problematic. Whether gross or subtle, your responses to such departures can maintain or increase the interaction difficulties.

Departures often involve either the dislocation of important personal level aspects from the clients' public level problems or else their public level activity being overturned and supplanted by a powerful personal level influence. Both of these circumstances can be construed as alterations in the client's public–personal equilibrium within the counselling transaction. If such occurrences are not recognized by the counsellor for what they are, they may be maintained or even amplified, unwittingly, by the counsellor's responses. As a result, significant shifts in the equilibrium may mean that the usually fluid movement between the interaction levels of the straightforward counselling transaction are replaced, either by a rigid mechanical and sterile exchange (public level dominance) or by a charged and uncontained emotional interchange (personal level dominance). Such disequilibrium can easily become established, resulting in a complicated counselling transaction.

You can learn to recognize the characteristic configurations of complicated counselling transactions by recognizing when and how you depart from your usual professional style or enter into one of the basic interaction patterns. Consequently, you may be in a position to predict and can sometimes usefully convey to your clients previously hidden aspects of their habitual interactive style, which are often part of their presenting problems as well as of your current pattern of interaction with them. This can importantly inform your subsequent management of the complicated counselling transaction (see Chapters 6, 7 and 8).

3

Counselling Transactions in Context

Your counselling transactions do not take place in a vacuum. As we described in the last chapter, you and your clients have histories which influence the present. In addition, the current relationships and responsibilities of each of you, for example as parent or employee, affect your capacity to carry out your respective roles within the counselling transaction.

Ideally, you and your clients' current interpersonal and social contexts are adequate to support the therapeutic endeavour. However, in practice, this may not be so. It is therefore important to understand the process by which the surrounding environment influences the counselling transaction. Studying such contextual influences can contribute to a more detailed assessment and evaluation of the ongoing transaction. Monitoring these influences helps you to foresee later complications and potentially to forestall them before they become too firmly established.

Accurately construing your clients' wider psychological and social contexts requires method. Considering your clients as belonging to a number of 'systems' can provide the necessary organizational framework. A system is defined as 'a whole composed of parts in orderly arrangement according to some scheme or plan, a set or assemblage of things connected, associated or interdependent, so as to form a complex unity' (*Shorter Oxford English Dictionary*: 2227).

Closed and open systems

In biology, sociology and other related sciences, the notion of a system has taken on a restricted and technical meaning (von Bertalanffy, 1973), which has been increasingly applied in the psychological field. Systems can be divided into two main types, closed and open. Closed systems are, at least theoretically, totally independent of their environment. Their initial condition is pre-determined and, like a battery cell, a closed system can be conceived as having 'gone flat', once it reaches its steady state. An open system, by contrast, is in constant contact with its environment. Through a process of dynamic exchange, referred to as homeostasis, an equilibrium is actively maintained. The living cell provides a good example of an open system which is dependent on its environment, reacting to it but simultaneously active in maintaining its integrity as a cell. The system of the counselling transaction is likewise dependent on its psychological and social environment, being affected by it but being required to maintain its integrity in order to function effectively to achieve its goals.

All systems that comprise people can be regarded as open systems. Thus individuals within a particular open system, such as a counselling transaction, are required, by the demands of their family or wider society (the surrounding supra-system), to function both as individuals and as part of a collective whole. Many people do not achieve this as it requires the ability to balance competing demands of various kinds which derive from membership of more than one system. The example of Helen, below, illustrates the implications for the counselling transaction system when the demands of a client's family system compete.

Helen, who left her therapy feeling that no progress had been made (page 13), wrote to her counsellor, apologizing profusely for her angry outburst and indicating how 'out-of-character' this was for her. She also requested a further appointment, which was duly made. When she re-presented, Helen appeared much more in control of herself. Falteringly, she talked of having been sexually abused by her deceased father and went on to describe her relationship with her mother, with whom she had continued to live. Helen and her mother had become increasingly mutually dependent on one another since her father's death. Although Helen felt trapped by her mother's dependence on her, the feelings of guilt,

which surfaced whenever she thought about leaving home,
prevented her from moving away.

Coming to the counselling sessions had amplified Helen's guilt
since she felt unworthy of obtaining help and also that getting
something for herself meant taking from her mother. This seemed
to be at least part of the reason that the counselling transaction had
been prematurely terminated. In a sense, the family system had
successfully competed with that of the counselling transaction.

Goals and demands of systems

Every system of which you are a member requires you to achieve a
particular goal or set of goals and, in this way, it makes demands on
you. As a child, within a 'normal' family system, you are expected to
keep to the standards of behaviour and rules imposed by its senior
and responsible members. Inevitably, as you get older, you join
other systems which, implicitly or explicitly, set you goals which
you need to attain to remain a member. Hence, schools set you
examinations to pass and your paid or unpaid work will require you
to carry out certain targets. You can elect to join some systems but
with others, like gender or ethnicity, you are a member irrespective
of your wishes. One implication of this is that some of the demands
imposed by systems are negotiable and others are non-negotiable.

The system of the counselling transaction

The counselling transactions which you and your clients enter into
are goal-oriented, even though the goals vary according to the
transaction and its stage. Often, within the two person system of
the transaction, your own goals and those of the client do not
conflict, although, as discussed earlier, this should not be assumed.
This is especially so where you have statutory responsibilities and
the clients may be subject to at least some degree of compulsion to
attend sessions with you.

Even when you have negotiated therapeutic goals with the
client, each of you may have subsidiary goals that are unknown to
the other but which you both nonetheless wish to achieve. These
can gain ascendancy during the counselling transaction and their
unspoken pursuit may be sufficient to undermine the public level
therapeutic goals by supplanting them or diverting time and energy
away from them.

Another way of looking at this situation involves the public and personal levels of interaction within the overall clinical transaction being construed as its 'sub-systems', which may have different goals from one another. When such goals compete or clash, problems may be generated, especially if your client cannot or will not differentiate between the two levels or sub-systems (see Chapters 1 and 2). Ideally, you and the client explicitly negotiate particular transaction goals, which are appropriate to your public level role responsibilities as counsellor. Any personal goals which remain hidden and un-negotiated may conflict with those in the public sub-system and have the potential to complicate the overall counselling transaction, especially if they are pursued at the expense of public level work, as can happen in many complicated counselling transactions. However, as with Malcolm, it may not be obvious, especially at the outset, that the goals of different sub-systems are competing within the counselling transaction.

Malcolm, who presented with problematic nightmares, did not comply with his counsellor's requests for him to keep a diary (page 3). He did not fulfil his role as a client appropriately, even after his counsellor's attempt to re-negotiate the trans-action goals. A more complete picture of the transaction's context, however, was not revealed to his counsellor until she received an unexpected telephone call from Malcolm's family doctor. The latter, obviously angry, told the counsellor about a recent visit to the Health Centre where Malcolm had physically threatened staff, after being offered a non-urgent appointment with the doctor. He had been forcibly removed from the Health Centre premises by police.

During the course of this informal case discussion, the doctor indicated that Malcolm was attempting to make exag-gerated claims for benefits to both Health and Social Services Departments and that his pregnant partner had served a prison sentence for fraud and theft. The doctor sounded annoyed at being involved in the financial claims for disability by both partners. To the surprise of the counsellor, the doctor stated that he thought counselling was making Malcolm more aggressive.

Through this unscheduled contact, Malcolm's counsellor under-stood more about the covert goals of her client's family system. She felt herself to be naïve to have taken Malcolm's public sub-system goals at face value. Malcolm's aberrant personal sub-system goals (involving the exaggeration of his medical and psychological status to boost his chances of state benefits) turned out to be strongly reinforced by those of his partner. Perhaps, not unreasonably, she was pressurizing him to provide a larger and more stable income to support their future child. Two of her previous children, by another partner, had been taken into local authority care. The conversation with the doctor meant that the counsellor's wider interpersonal environment (the quality of her relationship with the referring doctor) had changed, in that she felt stung by the doctor's criticism of her and unsupported by him.

Maintaining the integrity of a system
Achieving the goals of the counselling transaction system depends on many factors, including maintaining internal boundaries both within the transaction (between its public and personal sub-systems) and also with other external systems. You and your clients are required to balance your individual, public and personal sub-system needs and demands with those of your respective wider systems environment. Conflicting needs or demands, as in Malcolm's case, induce strain in the system of the transaction. Such strain may be sufficient to interfere with the integrity of the transaction so that it no longer achieves its goals.

In systems theory, different systems can either overlap or relate hierarchically to each other (see below). Furthermore, the goals and roles of different systems are not always compatible but may be conflicting or mutually exclusive. Such system theory viewpoints can provide a helpful perspective on how the effect of the inter-relationship of sub-systems, systems and supra-systems can complicate the counselling transaction.

The counselling transaction system of Malcolm and his counsellor and the influence of its relationship to its wider systems environment (Malcolm's partner and the Health Centre staff) demonstrates how the integrity of the various systems and sub-systems involved can be lost and the boundaries between them breached or, at least, blurred. Early in counselling, the personal sub-system between Malcolm and his counsellor intruded into their public sub-system, making it almost impossible to carry on the therapeutic work of addressing the problematic nightmares and anger. The integrity of the two-person system of the counselling transaction was also breached by the influence of Malcolm's partner and her financial scheming. The latter affected his personal motives for seeking therapy. This distorted the transaction via Malcolm's contribution to the personal sub-system. In a sense, the counsellor was being asked to deal with the couple's personal system agenda of obtaining increased 'benefit', which was not consonant with that of the stated public sub-system. The result was that the counselling transaction's public sub-system was inadequately supported by that of the personal and the integrity of the overall counselling transaction (supra-system) was consequently threatened.

The doctor's disclosures to the counsellor provide evidence of a breakdown in the integrity of professional relationships so that the boundary between the counselling transaction and the Health Centre systems was breached. It did not appear that there was sufficient justification for such a breach of confidentiality since the doctor, who might have appropriately warned the counsellor of her client's violent potential if he believed her personal safety was at risk, seemed only intent on complaining to her about Malcolm's mental state and, implicitly, about her incompetence as a counsellor.

Hierarchic systems

The system of the counselling transaction can be regarded as a subsystem of a higher system or supra-system, which in turn may be a sub-system of a still higher system. For example, the counselling transaction may be a sub-system of a Health Centre, Probation Service or Social Services supra-system, all of which are subsystems of the supra-system of Central Government (see Figure 3.1). Ideally, the goals of systems near the top of the hierarchy are consonant with, if not identical to, the goals of systems lower down. Even when the goals of the systems coincide, however, they tend to be translated into action in different ways, depending upon the hierarchic level of the system they belong to. The higher the system, the more its goals are achieved through management and strategic planning. Systems lower down the hierarchy tend to achieve goals practically, including through direct interaction with a client.

When the goals which arise from the set of systems to which you belong conflict with those from your clients' hierarchical systems, problems in maintaining the integrity between the open system of your transaction and that of other systems in the hierarchy may

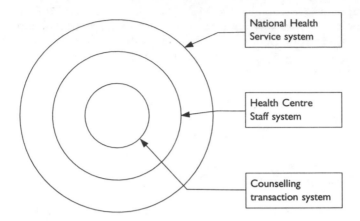

Figure 3.1   *Hierarchic systems*

result. These can induce strain in the transaction, potentially complicating it and impairing the quality of its outcome, as occurred
with Malcolm.

As Malcolm's counsellor was employed by the Health Centre she
was faced with conflicting goals and professional responsibilities.
She felt a responsibility to support Malcolm in meeting their
negotiated transaction goals, helping him with his anger and
nightmares, and believing in his personal integrity and honesty. As
an employee of the Health Centre she felt an obligation to a higher
system, which the family doctor partly embodied. In relation to this
higher system, she felt some responsibility for ensuring that scarce
financial and other resources should be apportioned fairly (part of
her public sub-system, social role responsibility) and felt angry
when she realized she might be colluding with an exaggerated or
fraudulent claim for benefits. However, she also felt undervalued
and misunderstood by the doctor (hence by the immediate supra-
system), believing his implied criticism of her to be quite unjustified.

Malcolm and his partner are also part of a hierarchy of systems,
although their membership is less conspicuous as, without paid
work, they are not part of a visible employment hierarchy. They
are, however, lower down the hierarchy with respect to the formal
systems of Central Government, for example, the Departments of
Health and Social Security. Although they can choose to be part of
some systems, such as the benefits system, membership of others

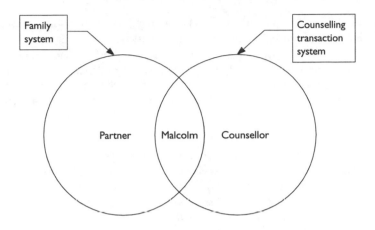

Figure 3.2 *Overlapping systems*

is non-negotiable, for example, that section of Social Services which has a statutory responsibility to monitor their parenting capacities. It is not difficult to see that the needs and demands of different levels in their hierarchy of systems could conflict.

Overlapping systems

You and your clients belong to family, community, ethnic group and other systems, some of which have a clear hierarchical relationship to one another, while others are much more horizontally related, referred to as overlapping (see Figure 3.2). In overlapping systems, which do not have fixed or clear hierarchies, each person can belong to more than one system and the demands of differing systems may either coincide or conflict. Thus the goals of the system of the counselling transaction with its implicit and explicit demands (for example, for attendance at appointments or prompt payment of bills for counselling) might conflict with those of the overlapping system of your clients' family which also requires the clients' presence and the prudent disposal of the family's finances.

In Malcolm's case, it appeared that he viewed the overlapping system of his relationship with his partner as being more important than the counselling transaction. With other clients, however, this may not be the case. Helen, although initially putting the demands of her family system before (hence above) her own, moved towards a less (or even inverted) hierarchical relationship as she attempted to put her own needs before those of her mother.

If you see that complications in the counselling transaction have arisen through the clash of competing goals from hierarchical and/ or overlapping systems, these can sometimes be usefully placed on the public agenda. They can thus become transaction goals or form the basis of a discussion during which further therapeutic goals can be identified.

> *When Helen re-presented to her counsellor it gave him an opportunity to complete his assessment. In particular, he was able to explore with Helen the ambivalence she felt about seeking help for herself. This stemmed from feeling guilty and her belief that obtaining help for herself was depriving her mother. Together they were able to discuss the requirements of the system of the counselling transaction and how far, realistically, these might impinge on those of her relationship with her mother, that is the family system.*

In such instances, the discussion can lead to people in the clients' wider social network becoming directly involved in their therapy or, in other instances, to their being educated about the needs and demands of counselling on the clients. The latter maximizes the chances that the support for the clients will be unambiguous. Later, we shall discuss the details of how to utilize the wider social network in your interventions (see Chapter 8).

Isomorphic systems

Applying systems theory allows an understanding of the phenomenon of 'isomorphism', which is relevant to some of the most difficult to manage and perplexing complicated counselling transactions. Isomorphism, which means 'having the same form', reflects the simultaneous enactment of a particular interactive aspect within a number of related systems, including that of the counsellor–client system and overlapping systems (sometimes, also including that of the supervisor–supervisee system, see Mattinson 1992). The result is a set of inter-related systems which resonate to the same dominant interaction theme.

> *Barbara's client, who had been sexually abused since the age of six by various men in her family, told Barbara that her*

mother had not believed her when told of the abuse. It was
following this rebuttal that she took her first overdose, using
her mother's contraceptive pills. Over the following few
sessions, Barbara's client discussed her concerns that her
youngest sister, now six years old, was currently being
abused by father. Her client confirmed, in a contemptuous
voice, that once more she had told her mother but that the
latter had again dismissed her worries as 'ridiculous'.

Barbara's client was also adamant that Barbara would not
take her concerns seriously, because she tended to view
Barbara, who was employed by Social Services, as an unhelp-
ful authority figure. Barbara privately felt insulted and hurt
by these remarks, which were repeated in succeeding sessions.
Barbara believed that, not only did she have a legal duty to
act on the information her client had provided, but she
needed to convince her client that she took the latter's needs
seriously. She thus discussed with her client her intention to
inform the relevant individuals within the Social Services.

Much to Barbara's surprise, the professional colleague she
spoke to seemed not to take the matter seriously, saying that
the whole of the client's family was regarded as too chaotic to
be able to make use of any help. A similar attitude was
detected in the policewoman who had been reluctantly
assigned to investigate the criminal aspects of the case.
Barbara felt shocked, angered and impotent, powerfully
realizing how her client must have felt not to be believed or
taken seriously by her mother. She now understood why her
client had not expected her to react any differently from her
mother.

Where other professionals and other agencies are involved with
your clients, knowing about isomorphism can be especially
relevant, since the identification of a dominant interactive theme
within the surrounding systems can reveal a current complication
within the counselling transaction hitherto hidden.

In the above example, the surprising reaction Barbara received
from professionals within her own overlapping systems left her
feeling unheard, frustrated and despairing. Barbara felt that the
other professionals minimized the seriousness of her client's
situation and dismissed the possibility that the family could use
help. This allowed them to distance themselves from experiencing

uncomfortable feelings of impotence, which, however, were all too painfully located in Barbara. Barbara felt she was the only one taking her professional responsibility seriously. She was then able to realize how her client must have felt when, behaving responsibly, she was still disbelieved by her mother. This realization allowed Barbara to make empathic contact with her client, at a deeper level than previously. Barbara felt this deeper understanding might not have been achieved had she herself not experienced the isomorphic phenomenon with her professional colleagues.

Attending to and resolving the interactive problem in one system, such as that between Barbara and her professional colleagues, can sometimes weaken the restricting psychological grip of the dominant interactive theme on the other isomorphic systems. This is evidence of the extent to which the isomorphic systems themselves are dependent upon one another for the maintenance of their overall stability. As a result of progress in the counselling transaction which followed Barbara's enhanced empathic contact with her client, her client decided talk to her mother again. Perhaps because they were voiced more convincingly or without so much venom, the mother was finally able to listen to the concerns of her daughter about the younger sister. For the first time the mother was able to verbalize her own concerns about her husband's demanding sexual behaviour. Eventually, the freeing up of the previously isomorphic systems led to the co-ordination of an inter-agency plan of action, involving all the relevant statutory services. However, this was only possible after the constituent systems stopped resonating to the isomorphic theme.

Releasing one system from the grip of a dominant theme may not only allow other systems to be freed but may also provide you with an opportunity for increasing your clients' insight into the wider significance of the theme. Some professionals routinely use this approach to understanding their therapeutic work, especially those working with abused and abusing families (Asen et al., 1989).

Summary

The relationships between people and groups of people can be viewed as interacting systems which behave in a limited number of predictable ways in relation to one another. Thus the relationship between you and your clients, the system of the counselling transaction, is influenced by many other systems both hierarchical and overlapping. Some of these will impose goals on or demand behaviour from either or both of you, such that they may compromise your ability or desire to carry out your responsibilities as dictated by the proper needs of the counselling transaction.

It is important to appreciate how the differing goals of various systems may either compete with or complement one another, especially if you have failed to find the source of the complicating influence by examining factors intrinsic to the counselling transaction. In earlier chapters we discussed how significant departures may arise from inappropriate role expectations, including the conflation of the role and the person and the influence of past relationships on the present transaction. The application of a system-based approach provides a third perspective from which to identify the source of the complicating factors. How the wider environment of your counselling transactions may be used to maintain their straightforward character or to resolve their complicating effects once established is discussed in Chapters 6 and 8.

4

Assessment for Counselling

The main aim of assessment is to form an opinion about your clients' capacity to engage with you in order to negotiate and pursue transaction goals, including that of successfully disengaging from your professional relationship. This means evaluating your clients' capacity to perform their expected role in relation to you and your actual circumstances, rather than to an idealized therapy and perfect setting. The task involves assessing your own capacities to carry out your professional role with each particular client. Such self-evaluation is intrinsically difficult, since knowing and respecting your own capacities, and the constraints they impose, are not easy.

In this chapter we shall consider how the assessment process can be used to predict later significant departures within the counselling transaction. This is not to assert that clients, with whom complicated transactions are likely to develop, should necessarily be regarded as unsuitable for counselling. You need to be aware, however, which of your potential counselling transactions are at special risk of becoming complicated.

It is not always possible, at assessment, to predict reliably which transactions will become complicated. We shall therefore consider some of the indications available during assessment, which suggest that the counselling transaction will remain straightforward. Thus, your assessment can include a consideration of both positive and negative factors in relation to predicting complicated transactions.

Standard procedure

Assessment not therapy

You are more likely to identify departures from the straightforward counselling transaction if the assessment process is repeatedly undertaken in the same thoughtful and ordered fashion. This does not have to mean that the assessment becomes mechanical or requires you to memorize a long list of questions, so that it degenerates into a 'question and answer' session. However, you have limited time at your disposal and are under some pressure to cover the most important and relevant avenues of enquiry. To an extent, therefore, you do attempt to cover much of the same ground with most of the clients you assess.

One practice, which can easily be incorporated into your usual assessment procedure, is to make a clear mental distinction about when the assessment phase has been completed and when you are actually starting counselling. Ideally, you should also make this distinction clear to your clients. They are then in no doubt about whether or not they have been offered a contract for counselling.

Helen's therapist, unsettled by his client's tears, failed to elicit relevant background details about her wider psychological and social context but drifted almost immediately into counselling. He had not explained to Helen that he needed to evaluate her suitability and that this would require him to know about, in some detail, particular aspects of her past and current life. He hurried to a premature formulation of her case and into a consequent 'therapeutic mis-alliance' (Meissner, 1993).

Multiple assessment interviews

Some important departures from the straightforward are subtle and only evidenced by the absence of particular features. For this reason, it can be helpful not only to standardize your assessment procedure, but to organize it into at least two sessions or parts. You can tell your clients that this is your usual practice and, if appropriate, explain your rationale to them (see Chapter 5). Dividing up your assessment phase helps you to identify those clients who are more likely and, importantly, those who are less likely to fulfil their role as clients adequately.

Even if your professional circumstances do not allow you to extend the time allocated for assessment, dividing your total time across two interviews or taking a break in the middle of a single interview can yield other dividends. You may well gain evidence of how much your clients have been able to assimilate emotionally and intellectually since your 'first' meeting. You can assess the extent to which they can recall what they regarded as the main elements of the earlier assessment and the degree to which these coincide with or are different from your view of the important themes. Furthermore, you can see if your 'first' interview has stimulated any psychologically minded curiosity or insight in your clients. Their failure to recall the assessment in any detail should signal concern and you need to set aside ample time to understand your clients' 'amnesia'. If there is little significant recall, if trivial or peripheral items are remembered at the expense of central ones, you should be alert to the possibility of later significant departures.

More than one assessment interview may reveal discrepancies or discontinuities in the content or emotional tone of your clients' narratives from your first to your second meeting. Even where the shift in tone is in a positive direction, from the first to the second interview, this should not be accepted unquestioningly. The matter should be raised on the public level agenda for discussion. If there is no evidence that your clients have psychologically processed material between sessions, any marked discontinuity or serious shift needs to be taken as predictive of later significant departures (see also Chapter 2, page 30).

Presentation of the problem

How and what your clients present to you as their problems, hence as potential public level therapeutic goals, may indicate whether they will have difficulty in adequately fulfilling their client role. Potential difficulties may be obvious, if these include an acknowledgement that there was previous failure to comply with professional advice or to complete a course of therapy. Often, however, you have no obvious clues. Instead, your clients might present a vague or non-specific complaint, such as 'just not feeling right'. Sometimes, complaints of 'boredom' or 'emptiness' may be prominent. In other cases there may be no complaint or presenting problem, but rather a general request for 'growth' or 'health'.

None of these diffuse presenting complaints or requests should be left without enquiry, nor should they be dismissed as insignificant simply because they are unclear. Their lack of clarity may be an important indicator of later significant departures but you should ascertain that your clients' vagueness of problem presentation is not a matter of their deliberate choice or personal style.

Although it seemed initially that Malcolm's only significant difficulties were his poor sleep and nightmares, his counsellor's efforts clarified some other daytime difficulties. He had not volunteered the existence of his violent daytime ideas as he felt embarrassed that they should cause him problems. This was partly because his partner had ridiculed him on account of them and he had felt humiliated. Malcolm thus had the necessary capacity to recognize his other difficulties but only once the reasons for his reticence had been aired and understood. His initial incomplete presentation of his problem was not, therefore, indicative of significant departures.

Your response to vague symptoms should be enquiries which aim to clarify and focus. When your clients use descriptive terms, such as 'boredom', 'anxiety' and 'depression', to refer to their complaints, you need to explore the meaning *they* attach to such terms, to minimize the confusion that can arise when technical terms are used idiosyncratically. You might say, 'Different people mean different things by "depression". Can you tell me what you mean?' Just because your clients use a term with which you are familiar, you should not assume that it has the same meaning for them.

Other clients may be unable to register their emotions or convey them in words, a condition known as alexithymia (literally meaning, no words for feelings (see Sifneos, 1973)). Undertaking psychological work with these clients is not only arduous but likely to yield significant departures since they have a profound deficit which will often impact negatively at the personal level interaction.

Clients with learning disabilities represent a client group whose specific cognitive difficulties may require you to spend time educating them as to what you expect of them in their client role, as part of clarifying the nature of their presenting problem. If you fail to do this or neglect to reassess frequently their public level understanding of the transaction, there may be significant departures (Sinason, 1992).

In some counselling transactions, even sensitive and relevant questioning fails to elucidate the presenting problem. One reason may be that the counsellor has focused on the presenting problems too prominently or too early in the assessment. Greater success can sometimes be achieved if this task is undertaken later in the interview, when any initial reticence or sense of strangeness may have diminished. It is, however, important for you to recognize and register any evidence of inappropriate problem presentation, thereby suggesting possible significant departures, and allow time to examine it, if necessary, later in the assessment.

Responsibility for the problem

In some clients who seek counselling, you identify a problematic emotion or behaviour, such as outwardly directed physical violence, which might predict later significant departures in the transaction. If so, it is important that you establish how much genuine responsibility they can accept for their part in the problem. If they exclusively blame other people or external agencies, they may have a seriously underdeveloped or impaired capacity to take appropriate responsibility or to construe accurately their own role in external events. Such clients often have a long-held belief that they are the hapless victims of a merciless world. Even though there may be some truth behind this, in that they have indeed suffered much adversity, their passionate commitment to this viewpoint means they are unlikely to pursue an appropriately active part in their client role (Sheila's counsellor was faced with this prospect at the outset). Raising this important issue on to the public level agenda is important since it can facilitate discussion, which may produce a further relevant goal for the transaction and may also encourage the client to interact more. When depression or inwardly directed violence, para-suicide, deliberate self-injury or severe addictive states are presenting problems, it is also important to ascertain the degree of responsibility your clients accept for these behaviours.

> *Initially, Barbara's client could accept little responsibility for her violence. When asked about her own part in it, she tended to rant about the way nobody ever listened to what she had to say. It was only after two years in counselling that she showed signs of being able to think about, thereby taking some responsibility for, her anger and its effect on others. This progress became evident during a phase when she spoke about previously feeling let down by her mother. Around the same time, she talked about fearing that her anger would drive away her current partner. She also started to recognize feelings of sadness and a dreadful*

sense of being entirely alone in the world, which she claimed
she had only ever before felt fleetingly.

Ownership of the problem can develop gradually during the course
of counselling, as above, and this is more likely if it has been one of
the negotiated therapeutic goals. Judging the authenticity of your
clients' communication about owning responsibility can be problematic. For example, if they have had contact with the criminal
justice system, they will have associated the admission of responsibility with being found guilty and punished. If they have had
previous counselling or psychotherapy, which has equipped them
with psychological jargon, their use of it may make them sound
falsely insightful.

> *Andrew had not had previous counselling but his intellectual*
> *and verbal skills made him appear 'insightful'. After listening*
> *to Andrew talking about his difficulties, his counsellor realized*
> *that all he was hearing was a detailed and eloquently*
> *presented list of established problems. During Andrew's pauses*
> *his counsellor felt, alternately, an internal pressure to solve*
> *Andrew's problems and make his life better or else a drive to*
> *disengage emotionally. As he noticed this repeatedly, his*
> *counsellor decided to explore with Andrew how much choice*
> *he had in talking and behaving in this way.*
>
> *Counsellor: I think you are trying hard to be helpful in telling*
> *me a lot of detail about your difficulties. You seem, however, to*
> *be giving me a longer and longer list, rather than thinking*
> *about any one difficulty in depth. It makes me wonder if this*
> *might be a way of avoiding uncomfortable feelings to do with*
> *looking at your part in generating these difficulties.*

Your intuition, together with evidence from appropriate prompts
or probing questions, as above, and attending to what your clients
say and how they say it, should help you to decide on the issue of
authenticity. As with Barbara's client, some people need a period
of successful counselling to achieve appropriate ownership of
responsibility for their presenting problems.

Realistically wanting to be rid of the problem

Frequently, clients present with little insight into the seriousness of
their problems and the likely difficulty involved in their solution.

Your clients' motives for coming to counselling will often involve a quest for increased self-knowledge or an acknowledgement of inadequate insight. However, lack of insight about the seriousness or the entrenched nature of the presenting problem, while not uncommon, may be a predicter of later significant departures. Your clients may also, like Andrew, believe that their problems will vanish simply by seeing a counsellor and without any active personal involvement in the therapeutic process.

Sometimes, even though symptoms or problems are presented, these do not seem to cause your clients any obvious anxiety or other psychic discomfort. The 'complaint' is made without conviction and you may be unable to detect a sense of concern in them (Norton, 1997). Even though you explore the situation with your clients (as did Andrew's counsellor), you may be unable to demonstrate that the 'complaint' causes your clients any emotional pain. Your clients communicate the difficulty with no discernible personable level component. Your attempts to forge a link with your clients' personal level are either unemotionally dismissed or alternatively met with obvious belligerence, deriving from a sense of personal indignation. Both responses provide evidence of your clients' public–personal disequilibrium. What you do not gain from either response is any real sense of why there is a lack of emphasis or conviction. They do not, for example, indicate that they are unwilling or afraid to talk to you, a relative stranger, about a sensitive issue as they imagine this would leave them feeling both exposed and vulnerable. They can only dismiss your enquiry as fatuous or become enraged at having to account for their attitudes (Kernberg, 1989).

In extreme instances, your clients will appear emotionally unaffected, even by the seriously aggressive or irresponsible behaviour about which they tell you (see Chapter 9). They may strive to justify such behaviour but their justifications are delivered divorced from any emotion, with an intimidating edge or in a righteously indignant manner. Barbara's client, for example, ignored Barbara's initial enquiry about her violence, giving Barbara an icy stare and carrying on talking about how let down she felt when her sexual partners inevitably 'abandoned' her. In such instances, your clients display no real concern for others, even those who have been at the receiving end of their past physical or mental abuse. Counselling transactions with such clients are likely to become complicated.

In some transactions, the absence of concern is not so easy to detect, particularly when you find the presented problematic behaviour, for example, violence or sexual perversion, to be personally distasteful to you. It can be difficult to decide the extent to which your clients can hold any appropriate concern for others, when you are struggling to feel any empathy with them at all. Such a situation calls for close monitoring of your own public–personal equilibrium, lest a personal aspect of your own complicates the counselling transaction. Again, there is a strong likelihood that transactions with such clients will become complicated.

Multiple presented problems
Multiple problems presented at assessment can signal a likely complicated transaction, especially but not exclusively, if your clients' complaints are vague or diffuse (Brooke, 1994). The more major the problems (such as binge-eating, self-induced vomiting, purgative misuse, promiscuity, sleep disorder, para-suicide or drug addiction) your clients bring, the more likely your transaction is to become complicated, as such behaviours are often aspects of a severely disordered personality (see Chapter 9) which can contribute to departures in both the public and personal levels of your interaction (Norton, 1996).

None of these features in isolation, however, are contra-indications to agreeing to work with clients but rather they suggest the likelihood of later complications arising. Each feature needs to be considered in the context of your assessment of your clients' overall interaction with you.

Disclosure of personal information

A strong predictor of later significant departures is that your clients find it difficult to move, within the transaction, from the public level into the realm of personal feelings and motives and vice versa. In the majority of straightforward counselling transactions, by contrast, your clients present their complaints or problems as coming 'from within' themselves (Brooke, 1994), signifying that their public level capacity to be a client is adequately supported by and integrated with their personal realm. They may also demonstrate an ability to balance the expression of their public and personal level needs with an awareness of your professional requirement to make an assessment. They accept that, within prescribed limits, you will put yourself professionally at their disposal and not deliberately and unhelpfully interpose any of your own concerns or views.

Characteristically, the narratives of these clients are coherent. If there are inconsistencies in their accounts of their own or their family histories, they become understandable through additional questioning. Furthermore, these clients demonstrate an ability to think about contradictions in their accounts and provide credible reasons for them which move the assessment forward. Your overall impression of the assessment is that your clients have been able to present a progressively more complex, 'three-dimensional' representation of themselves and their interpersonal relationships.

Other counselling transactions, even with prompting or coaxing, lack this characteristic. Your clients are unable to respond to your cues and questions so that your assessment does not gain in clarity or depth. Indeed, your clients' answers may only further obfuscate the situation, which becomes more confused with further enquiries (Kernberg, 1975). When this happens you may be tempted to change your line of enquiry and it may be appropriate to do so. However, you need to register the fact of the obfuscation, since, if it is repeated, it may generate significant departures. Some clients are unable to bring personal level material into the interaction, while others are not able to differentiate between the more personal level of disclosure and their presented public level problems. They tend to present 'of' themselves rather than 'from within' themselves (Brooke, 1994).

Malcolm's almost relentless presentation of his violent thoughts speaks of his incapacity to differentiate his role as client from his problematic personal self. He is unable to stand back from this problem and discuss the situation with his counsellor. He cannot say 'I have thoughts of terrible violence and am terrified that one day I might act on them and injure somebody very badly'. Such a statement would allow his counsellor to both reflect on the nature and severity of her client's problems and decide how best she might be able to help him. Instead, Malcolm simply repeats the problem, over and over, as if this were the only way he could convince her and himself of the genuineness of his need for help. In this way, he presents 'of' rather than 'from within' himself.

Family background

At assessment, many clients volunteer little about the quality and nature of their interpersonal relationships, past or present. One of your tasks, therefore, is to establish which of a variety of reasons accounts for such omission. First, your clients may not consider the relationships important or relevant to the assessment. Secondly, they may deliberately avoid the topic since the attendant emotions, such as anger, shame, depression and guilt, which such a revelation might evoke, are imagined to be unbearable. Thirdly, little memory may exist of details of past relationships, making recall impossible. You need to establish the reasons for the lack of presented information since these have differing implications for predicting later significant departures. Noting your clients' responses to your enquiries about these omissions may also inform your assessment. Pronounced defensiveness, such as repeatedly avoiding the topic or irritable and hostile responses, strengthen your prediction.

Some clients concentrate exclusively on the presenting problems with a concomitant reluctance to give historical information regarding past problems. Less commonly, they adopt an avoidant strategy by focusing on a past problematic relationship, for example one that involved childhood sexual abuse, thus excluding a relevant discussion of current problems. Both of these stances, although subtle, can signal later significant departures and are important to detect and explore in order to assess the extent to which your clients can recognize and take responsibility for their avoidant strategies.

Your questioning will be directed by a consideration of what you think has been omitted. You should not initially accept an explanation of simple amnesia, or your clients' opinions that such information is irrelevant, until you have pursued the matter further. You may need to tell your clients of your view that focusing on one particular topic is an avoiding tactic and that you need to understand their reasons for this stance and also to ascertain whether they can relinquish this position.

Clients who have experienced extreme deprivation or neglect may have few early family memories and may even report unremarkable childhoods. Such reports, however, usually lack corroborating detail and are characteristically bland, being also devoid of positive details. You may need to enquire more directly as to the possibility of gross early deprivation, if other avenues of questioning have proved unproductive in clarifying the lack of detail in your clients' early relationships.

Clients who are likely to be able to maintain a straightforward counselling transaction are able to talk about past and present key figures in a way which conveys them to be real people. This ability is not solely dependent upon your clients' intellectual or educational level, and clients whose vocabularies are poor for a variety of reasons, such as low intellect or inadequate formal education, still may provide convincing accounts. A realistic account usually contains sufficient detail to allow you to form a fairly full picture of your clients' significant relationships. It often involves your clients discussing their ambivalent feelings towards, or apparent inconsistencies or contradictions in, their carers' personalities. These will be discussed in a balanced way with your clients demonstrating a capacity to identify and evaluate positive and negative aspects of the relationships in a coherent and consistent manner. Such a capacity, however, is often not present in your clients during assessment.

A capacity to think about and discuss the impact of another's thoughts and actions upon you implies a capacity to see yourself separate from but in relationship to the 'other'. Consequently, if this is so, your clients have probably developed a mature capacity to withstand psychological and physical separation from the 'other' and are able to sustain mentally the relationship during actual periods of separation, although such separations may engender feelings of anxiety, anger, sadness and loneliness (Bowlby, 1973). In the assessment situation, however, you may need to ask directly about your clients' reactions to and thoughts about important separations and losses during childhood and adulthood, rather than to assume that they will spontaneously volunteer the information or that they will have been able to deal maturely with these life events.

Other pointers towards future significant departures include your clients' descriptions of significant figures in their lives in either consistently glowing or consistently derogatory terms. There are no shades of grey, such as contradictions or other reported imperfections in your clients' descriptions, which would portray a more human picture of these people. Of similar importance is when your clients describe a person in totally contradictory ways, within the same interview or even more strikingly, within seconds. Such inconsistencies may be associated with later significant departures. First of all, however, you need to ascertain that your clients are unable to acknowledge the presence of, or satisfactorily account for, the contradiction when it is brought to their attention. If your clients either change the subject or their narratives become markedly incoherent, when you are seeking clarification, they may have a seriously compromised capacity to fulfil their role as a client in a straightforward manner.

> *During the course of the initial assessment interview Peter's client told him about his jealous feelings towards his wife. He spoke critically of her weak and fickle character, while at other times he showered her with praise. After this had occurred a few times Peter decided to draw this apparent contradiction to his client's attention.*
>
> *Peter: You have told me quite a lot about your wife but I am a bit confused. Sometimes you describe her as 'all bad'. At other times you seem to say she is 'nothing but good'. Can you shed any light on this?*
>
> *After a few seconds silence, Peter's client left the room saying he needed to use the toilet. When he returned he began to talk about his minor 'cannabis habit'. Peter attempted to explore his client's view of his wife and also his avoidant reaction to Peter's comment. The latter's repeated attempts were greeted by his client continually changing the topic of conversation. Peter took this as evidence of his client's impaired capacity to fulfil the client role adequately.*

At one moment, the emotional tone of your encounter may be negative and the next positive, or vice versa, as with Peter and his client (see Chapter 1). Ideally, you will mentally note the abrupt and extreme shift in the emotional climate at the personal level inter-action and bring it to the public level agenda for further discussion. This may be difficult, especially if, like Peter, you are feeling confused and emotionally battered by your client's volatility. You may be tempted to avoid further exploration, especially if the climate shifts from negative to positive, because of feeling relief in the more relaxed atmosphere. You need to be aware, however, that this feeling of relative calm may only be a lull before the next storm. It is important to recognize the presence of these shifts, more than their content, as it signals your clients' difficulties in holding a coherent and stable emotional view of themselves and others.

'Deep' disclosure

One of the pitfalls awaiting the unwary or inexperienced coun-sellor is mistaking early and 'deep' disclosure of the clients' innermost personal details as genuine openness or enthusiasm for counselling. Such disclosure is likely to represent your clients' diminished capacity to be appropriately private. Healthy privacy requires a self-imposed public–personal boundary, evidenced by gradual self-disclosure which deepens, over time, with the development of genuine rapport. The absence of healthy privacy, so that personal level issues constantly swamp the transaction, should alert you to the possibility of a later significant departure.

It is important that you register your reactions to clients' early and extensive revelations of 'deep' feelings, images or impulses. Your capacity to do this will critically depend on deciding whether in fact you have a mutually developed deep rapport or have simply been tempted to believe that you are especially skilful in having so quickly elicited these aspects from your clients. Succumbing to the view that you have a special flair for counselling the particular clients who provide such 'deep' expression very early on, or feeling more than usually skilful with particular clients (hopefully an unusual aspect of professional style for you), may be a response to your clients' idealization.

When your clients idealize you, it may be obvious but this is not necessarily so. You may only recognize the presence of idealization through identifying your inflated view of yourself, evidence of a departure from your usual view of yourself. Such idealization is often, although not always, precarious and may readily give rise, in turn, to profound denigration. If the former becomes established, it may represent the precursor of a strong erotic attachment which can be difficult to dismantle. Such a stable idealization can also degenerate quickly and dramatically into extreme denigration if it is questioned or otherwise eroded. The latter may also become established and can be of sinister, even dangerous, significance.

In some instances, idealization is stably maintained but at the price of hidden denigration, which is enacted elsewhere. Barbara's client, for example, told Barbara that she felt more comfortable talking to her than she ever had with anyone else. Almost immediately, however, she was raging against her family doctor. Ironically, it was he who had made the referral to Barbara. This doctor, according to the client, 'never listened and never understood anything'. Detecting such an attitude requires you to notice the tell-tale signs of idealization and then to be alert to the devaluation or denigration of others – 'friends' of the clients, professionals, or institutions such as the health service or counselling organizations with whom your clients have current or have had prior contact. Sometimes, your clients' idealized view of you is maintained at the expense of their view of themselves – one of self-loathing which they feel is entirely justified. If not part of a psychotic mental illness, when self-loathing may be present as part of a delusion of guilt or badness, self-hatred tends to be associated with ruthless feelings which may be manifest in a variety of self-harming, risk-taking or anti-social activities and behaviour (Brooke, 1994). Clients displaying such behaviours are seldom simple to deal with and are especially likely to become involved in complicated counselling transactions.

> *Towards the end of their second assessment interview, Peter's client told him that when he left the care of Social Services, at sixteen, he had drifted into drug addiction, a habit he supported by working as a male prostitute. His fresh complexion made him particularly popular with some of his 'clients' and, over the following four years, he formed a small number of enduring relationships with older males. When he reached adulthood he felt attracted to women and suffered his first depressive episode. He short-circuited his depressive feelings, however, when he found that self-mutilation lessened these painful emotions. Although he realized that scarring himself visibly kept the amorous advances of others at bay, he was less aware that this mechanism was his maladaptive attempt to solve his own internally conflictual feelings about his sexual orientation. Consequently, Peter's client did not view his self-harmful attacks as problematic. Indeed, he felt he did not deserve to lead a better socially adapted life.*

Peter viewed his client as having extremely low self-esteem, sometimes amounting to self-loathing, but at the time had detected no signs of mental illness, specifically no delusions.

Withstanding the demands of counselling

An important component of the assessment of the public and personal interactions between you and your clients is your judgement about the safety of the counselling transaction. You need to have considered whether there are risk factors to be inferred from the clients' histories, their current situation or the physical environment you meet in, which may destabilize your counselling transaction so that it becomes unsafe for you, your clients or others.

Table 4.1 *General considerations when assessing risk (adapted from the Royal College of Psychiatrists' Special Working Party on Clinical Assessment and Management of Risk, 1996)*

1 Risk cannot always be accurately predicted.
2 Risk cannot be completely eliminated.
3 Good assessment results in more effective risk management.
4 Risk is dynamic, depending on the person *plus* the circumstances.
5 As circumstances alter, your assessment must be frequently reviewed.
6 Interventions can increase as well as decrease risk.
7 Clients who pose risks to others often present risk to themselves.

This task overlaps with that of your assessment of your clients' psychosocial adjustment, their support network and the practical information you may obtain or request regarding their behaviour and reactions between sessions (see Chapter 5). At this point, however, we are interested in how, by monitoring the public and personal levels of interaction, you examine aspects which might indicate future dangerousness in your counselling transaction.

Even though it is impossible to make totally accurate predictions, there are some general important points worthy of consideration when you need to assess or manage dangerous situations (see Table 4.1).

Crucial to this endeavour of assessing risk is understanding the psychological, social and biological elements which may precipitate violent behaviour, as well as any predisposing factors. Sometimes, the risk of violent behaviour is general. At other times, it is focal and the result of unique trigger factors, sometimes specifically associated with an identified victim. Peter's client still harboured feelings of revenge against his foster father, who had sexually abused him when he was under his supposed parental care. These remained even though his foster father was dead, and Peter's client had already served a prison sentence for causing grievous bodily harm to him. Peter's view was that his client did pose some risk of violence to others, but that this was much less a risk than he would have posed had his foster father still been alive.

Table 4.2 lists some indicators of risk which you will need to have evaluated during your assessment and, where appropriate, during the counselling itself. A previous history of violence may strongly predict future violence, whether or not the violence was apparently unprovoked or callously calculated. However, merely

Table 4.2   *Factors indicating risk (adapted from Coid, 1996)*

History:
1 Previous violence or suicidal behaviour.
2 Unstable interpersonal and work relationships.
3 Evidence of poor compliance with any previous treatment or counselling.
4 Presence of substance misuse, alcohol and/or drugs or other disinhibiting factors, such as a social background promoting violence.
5 Any changes in mental state or behaviour, such as abnormal beliefs or experiences occurring prior to the violent behaviour.

Environment:
6 Evidence of recent severe stress, especially loss or the threat of loss, including loss of family or social support or accommodation.
7 Ease of access to potential victims identified in the clients' current psychological state assessments.

Psychological state:
8 Clients' declared intentions and attitudes to previous and potential victims.
9 Clients' specific threats.
10 Clients' ability to forward plan realistically.
11 Clients' capacity to tolerate frustration and manage impulse control.
12 Presence and strength of emotions related to violence, such as irritability, anger, hostility or suspiciousness.
13 The presence of symptoms suggestive of active mental illness, such as delusions, especially persecutory beliefs or delusions of mind or body being controlled or interfered with by external forces.

eliciting a history of violence is only a starting point. You need to gain an understanding of your clients' biographies and violent or offending behaviour from their own perspective. In other words, the world has to be viewed through your clients' eyes and their histories. Violent behaviour and its context have to be understood in this way, as well as in terms of external factors (Grounds, 1995). You need to ascertain whether your clients knew in advance that they would be violent, how driven they felt by painful or intolerable feelings and what, if anything, stopped them from being still more violent. Beware of minimizing the seriousness of any anti-social or violent behaviour just because it has not resulted in much physical damage or only resulted in damage to property rather than to people. A pitfall to avoid is looking disproportionately at the results of a violent action as opposed to looking more discerningly at the intensity of the feelings and thoughts fuelling the actions of your clients. Most importantly, you need to know about your clients' current views of any previous violence and whether they appreciate the need for external help, and what their attitude is towards people, such as yourself, who may be in a position to supply such help. If you embark on counselling without obtaining and considering this information, you may unwittingly provoke an emotional and behavioural response from your clients which puts yourself and others at risk.

Even if you work in a setting with generous support, both physical and psychological, and feel able to engage in complicated counselling transactions which are potentially dangerous or, in other ways, 'risky', it is our view that, you should carefully consider your professional and personal motives for doing so. You will need to ensure that you have adequate supervision. If you do undertake such work, you will need to evaluate continually the quantity, as well as quality, of support and protection available, and establish that it will be continuously present, both during the time of your sessions and for the total duration of the counselling transaction.

When there is any violence in your clients' past (including violence to property and self as well as to others) and the continuing presence of predisposing or particular trigger factors which signal the probability of recurrence, you need to pay serious attention to your clients' capacity for exerting impulse control. This needs to be considered and assessed in the context of the likely effects of psychological exploration, both intellectual and emotional, which will occur during the counselling transaction. However, even in those clients who have a clear history of violence, such as Barbara's client, there are few absolute contra-indications to therapy. With all clients you need to take into account factors which are specific to them and your setting, including your own capacities and skills and those elements which you can introduce to support and protect your work and which may also mitigate against future violence.

Monitoring the counsellor's personal reactions

In certain situations, it is especially hard to identify departures from the straightforward transaction. First, you may have unduly positive feelings which you can easily mistake for 'ordinary' job satisfaction, an elusive element in much counselling and psychotherapy! Secondly, there may be a relative absence of emotional contact with your clients, or difficulty in concentrating and finding yourself more readily distracted than usual. Thirdly, you may feel a certain blandness or emptiness to which, initially, you attach no importance. Fourthly, any of the above feelings may be associated with intense emotions or dramatic fantasies about your clients which arise only between sessions, including immediately after a session or immediately before the next session. Having at least two assessment sessions can help to facilitate the identification of these otherwise elusive or subtle signs which may predict later serious complications.

The key to understanding much of what transpires in the assessment phase, in terms of predicting later significant departures, lies in recognizing your own reactions (see Chapters 2 and 7). In effect, you act as a kind of psychological barometer, sensing even small or apparently trivial fluctuations in the public and personal level atmospheres, as well as any difficulty in moving between the levels or, alternatively, in maintaining the two levels as separable entities. Sifting evidence from all these sources will help you predict later significant departures. The direction of your prediction may fluctuate during the course of the assessment. In effect, you need to judge whether significant risk factors have accrued which indicate significant departures and consequently whether or not it is wise for you to offer therapy. Monitoring of this kind needs to continue throughout the entire course of the transaction, not solely during the assessment phase (see Chapters 6, 7 and 8).

A standard procedure for assessment facilitates your detection of both public and personal level fluctuations, that is departures from the straightforward counselling transaction. Within the public level interaction you should register even trivial departures because if any are ignored or considered insignificant, the cumulative total is underestimated and the overall predictive accuracy of anticipating a complicated transaction is diminished. Consequently, significant departures can surface 'out of the blue', as if without foundation and sometimes with disturbing or dangerous results.

Peter realized he had not fully explained the purpose and procedure of the assessment interview to his client. He omitted to tell him about its expected duration and that he would feel obliged to report any concerns he had about his client's violent potential to other colleagues. Peter was preoccupied by preparations for his own approaching holiday, although he could not know whether or not these public level lapses accounted for his client's departure in performing his role straightforwardly. Peter realized, however, that there might have been other departures from his own public level routine which he had not detected but which might have had a cumulative influence in complicating the transaction through his client not receiving the usual amount of orientating information and structure at the start of the interview.

You may already be aware that your feelings vary towards different clients, their age, gender, race, culture, physical attractiveness and social status evoking different personal responses from you. Nevertheless, within these 'categories', you will tend to recognize, on reflection, a usual range of emotional reactions. In some transactions, however, your clients' difficulties and behaviour elicit an unusual reaction in you. It is important to pay particular attention to such exceptions. Hence, if you habitually feel awkward when faced with your clients' tears, except on a particular occasion, note the context of this aspect of the interaction carefully. If you usually feel anxious or frightened in the presence of a client's direct expression of anger but do not on one particular occasion, it is important to register this as evidence of a serious departure, even though the realisation of the departure is only fleetingly present. Likewise, if you are less affected by your clients than usual, this is a departure from your own 'norm' and, as such, may signal that the transaction is becoming complicated. Sometimes, the departure from the straightforward counselling transaction is reflected in the interview progressing more smoothly than usual.

It may be difficult to find sufficient time to complete the assessment during the usual length of time you spend with your clients, although you sense you have worked at the usual rate and in the usual manner. You need to register such a situation as possibly signifying a departure, not that it is inevitably significant. It reflects a disturbance of the usual internal public–personal equilibrium within your straightforward counselling transaction, representing a relative shrinking of the public contribution to the interaction and an expansion of the personal. Construed in this way you can consider whether and how to respond, and decide whether to deviate deliberately from your usual practice or wait and attempt to understand further why the departure has occurred. This topic, of how to intervene, will be covered later in more detail (see Chapters 6 and 7).

Summary

Counselling transactions can become complicated for a variety of reasons, only some of which are apparent during your initial assessment phase. Your main task is to structure your assessment interview(s) so that you can reliably identify complicating factors in your clients, yourself and your respective wider social settings, including the physical setting in which the transaction takes place. Identifying departures from the straightforward counselling transaction or potential complicating factors in some clients should not automatically disqualify them from receiving counselling. Rather, the aim of your assessment is to promote an early recognition of such influences so that their deleterious effect, in producing later established complications of the transaction, can be minimized. You may decide, weighing the evidence, that clients with many significant departures will be suitable for counselling or, if not, you may wish to refer them elsewhere for a more appropriate intervention.

Structuring the assessment, for example by standardizing your procedure, utilizing more than one assessment interview and being clear when you are assessing and when counselling proper has begun, can increase your capacity to identify reliably departures or other potentially complicating factors at an early stage. Many relevant indicators of future significant departures stem from a public–personal disequilibrium. Sometimes this is obvious, especially when it is manifested in the clients, as with Barbara's client. When this is not the case, it is important that you try to identify when *you* depart from your own public and personal level norms in either quantity or quality. This is not easy and, for example, Barbara was initially quite unaware of any such departure in herself. She did not recognize that her own public–personal equilibrium had been disturbed. Overall, evidence of factors likely to complicate the transaction should influence but not dictate your decision to start counselling with particular clients.

Ideally, in the straightforward counselling transaction, the process of moving between public and personal levels is enriching, creating an ever more complex but understandable and deep representation of your clients' problems as they appear both in the counselling interaction and in their wider psychosocial environment. This is not always the case, however, since many straightforward counselling transactions will depart frequently and seriously, though not ultimately significantly or non-transiently.

Those clients who present 'of' themselves are particularly likely to induce complicated transactions. With them it may be difficult either to move between the public and personal interaction levels, as you make your assessment, or else to find evidence of their capacity to distinguish between the two levels. In some transactions this is indicated by a resistance to move to a more emotionally revealing level. In others, it is indicated by a plunging into the personal level with little or no capacity to regain or to participate in the necessary public level work which would allow accurate identification and owning of the presenting problem. In such transactions you may find that you have departed from your usual routine of assessment, that is at your public level, or reacted in a way which differs from your usual emotional disposition, that is at your personal level.

5

Practical Points: from Beginning to End

Some of the ideas introduced in earlier chapters now need to be discussed in terms of translating them into action so they may influence your everyday counselling practice. Our emphasis in this chapter is on how to keep in mind the interactive focus and overall context of the counselling transaction throughout its duration, which, of course, starts even before you and your clients meet in person.

Not all the relevant issues discussed will be equally applicable to all counsellors. And since a large number of factors, for example, gender, setting (home-based or office-based), level of protection (in terms of presence of other staff, use of 'alarms', self-defence training, etc.) are influential, there is not room to discuss each of these factors individually. Many of the points raised, however, are relevant to most counsellors.

The referral process and beyond

Barbara felt disturbed when she read the referrer's account of her clients' childhood sexual and physical abuse and adulthood sadistic violence. She felt alternately aggrieved for and angry with her client whom she had not met at this stage. For a day or so she found herself intermittently musing about these aspects but did not consider them in depth until the day of the assessment interview. Then she realized that she felt unusually anxious about the forthcoming meeting with her client and (more worryingly to her) she believed she was not going to be able to help her.

At the start of the referral process, both you and your clients may entertain many expectations, wishes and fears of one another, only some of which are likely to be realized in the ensuing transaction. Those which are not realized may generate later disappointment or frustration. On occasions you may observe your clients' reactions to feeling let down; at other times, these reactions remain covert. The more they remain covert the more are they likely to complicate the counselling transaction.

As well as being aware of the interactive focus throughout the entire counselling transaction, you need to consider the psychosocial environment in which the transaction takes place. In many instances this remains relatively static and stable. However, if changes do occur, such as the beginning or ending of an important relationship or a change of job, they can exert a potentially complicating influence. Some events are obvious and have clear emotional significance, for example, a death in the family or imprisonment. Others are much less so, such as an enforced consulting room change which may seriously upset some clients. Thus, events may have unforeseen or distant effects which in turn may have a complicating effect on your transaction. Sometimes, your clients do not tell you about a crucial 'external' event of theirs and the departure from the straightforward is the first, albeit indirect, evidence of the event. Information may be deliberately withheld from you by some clients but often their silence may reflect an unawareness of the emotional significance of an event.

> *Sheila eventually began counselling but for a long time remained unforthcoming, usually sitting with her back to her counsellor and avoiding eye contact with her at all other times. After attending regularly for over a year, she revealed that six months previously she had undergone a 'termination of pregnancy'. Sheila's counsellor was astounded on hearing this news since, as far as she had been aware, Sheila's life was particularly devoid of relationships, except those with her mother and brother. There had never been any mention of a man, let alone of a sexual relationship!*

You need to be aware of changes in your own wider psychosocial context which, without you realizing it, may exert an effect which complicates the overall transaction. As with your clients, these factors may be more or less obvious. In particular, you need to be aware when such factors resonate with your clients' presented problems, for example, if you are providing marital counselling while struggling with your own marital problems or dealing with issues concerning parenting or infertility while pregnant.

Tensions in both your immediate and wider work environment can be influential. They vary in significance and intensity and you may not always be fully aware of the extent to which you are affected by them. Sometimes these tensions derive from trivial 'tiffs' with colleagues, while others arise from more serious influences, for example, those involving vicissitudes in the government's or society's attitude to your profession, adverse media attention, legislative changes with relevance for your statutory duties, newsworthy items which relate to your clients as a group, especially where this is characterized by criminal activity.

> *Peter was alarmed to hear, on the radio, details of an assault which were uncannily similar to those his client had described when talking about his revenge attack on his late foster father. Moreover, the reported victim had been a convicted paedophile whose legal case had previously been much publicized by the media and who lived near Peter's client. Peter wondered if all of this were mere coincidence. He found himself dreaming that his client was being violent and, for a period, repeatedly woke up in the middle of the night in an anxious state.*

To take part in a complicated counselling transaction is not a crime and, in any case, the nature of much therapeutic work involves deviations from the 'straight and narrow' ideal world of theory. You are not required to behave like a computer, a robot or to be a super-human. With certain clients you will want to, and indeed circumstances may dictate that you do, deviate from your usual professional practice. Such departures, however, should be countenanced with care. The reasons for any excursion from your usual attitudes and behaviour need to be understood. Repeated deviations should be very carefully scrutinized to ensure that any consequent 'action' on your part is justified by the therapeutic situation. Helen's therapist, for example, might have done well to consider how far from his usual assessment style and practice he had allowed himself to stray.

Referral route

The process and content of the referral may indicate something about your potential clients and their context that may predict significant departures. Some routes are direct and simple, for example, the referrer is clear about the rationale for referring and knowledgeable about counselling, and sometimes also knows about your capabilities, interests and the setting in which you practise. Other referrals are protracted or circuitous. They convey to you a catalogue of failed engagements and premature terminations with previous therapists or counsellors but lack relevant personal information about your clients, especially regarding aspects of their histories and current difficulties.

> *After the telephone conversation (see page 35) Malcolm's counsellor realized that the family doctor who had referred Malcolm had known for some time about both the exaggerated benefits claims and the conflict in Malcolm's relationship with him. In spite of working in the same building as the referring doctor, this information had not been passed on. Although she felt sympathy for the hard-working doctor, the counsellor felt resentment that he had not been more thoughtful and thorough in making the referral.*

A referral route which has been tortuous and time-consuming adds to the likelihood that the eventual transaction will become complicated, since the reasons for the delays may recur, albeit in a different guise, within your own transaction. If your clients do not mention any frustration with the delays in the referral process, you should raise this possibility in your assessment. You may wish to comment on previous delays and acknowledge that your clients' referral to you may have evoked further discomfort and impatience. Sometimes there is a psychodynamic theme which is enacted at each stage of a protracted referral process. Identifying such a theme may be difficult but its discovery may protect your transaction from future significant departures deriving from a similar source (see also, isomorphism in Chapter 3).

> *To the outside world, the first obvious clues that all was not well with Barbara's client appeared when she was aged eleven years. They were noted by her form teacher who observed her marginalized position in the class. She was noted to be reluctant to change into her sports kit in front of*

other girls and her academic performance was much poorer than at her previous school, although this was not reported as such for two years. When recognized, educational psychologists became involved but by this time (aged thirteen) her position had changed from withdrawn outsider to troublemaker and daredevil, attracting a loosely aggregated gang of schoolgirl followers. Another year passed before the school's counsellor was involved. The referral to Barbara, once more involved a significant delay.

It can be useful to begin to think about your clients prior to your first interview. Sometimes you can collect extra information from the referrer about the referral route which can reveal interesting repetitive patterns. In the case of Barbara's client, the time delay following the recognition of her problems was the recurrent 'theme'. Privately, Barbara believed that the delays might be the result of institutionalized racism, since her client, like herself, was from an ethnic minority.

Investigation into the mechanics and duration of the referral process sometimes uncovers the unexpected involvement of other professionals with your clients. This knowledge can help you to assess more accurately your clients' wider psychosocial contexts, which are important if you are undecided about whether their social network can support them during the rigours of counselling.

Referral source
You will need to decide whether you are prepared to accept clients as self-referrals. This avoids some of the disadvantages of third-party referrals, including the need to liaise with other professionals and frustrating bureaucratic delays. However, such short-term advantages need to be set against the disadvantages which arise from an absence of sufficient or corroborated information about your clients. (This is especially relevant to counsellors working from their own homes or in other relatively 'unprotected' work settings.) You can easily become totally reliant on your clients' account, whether this is in relation to their problems, histories, needs or their wider contexts. Although comprehensive and perfectly corroborated information is unattainable, there are steps which you can take to validate your existing knowledge. Confirming the authenticity of your 'data', as well as obtaining

collateral information, is especially important if you are working in forensic or probation settings, or with clients where there is an elevated risk of dangerous behaviour. It is necessary, therefore, that you establish what you need to know about your clients and who you need to hear it from. Often you will need to discuss such aspects with your clients and obtain their permission to contact others about them.

Self-referrals place you at potentially the greatest disadvantage in terms of quality of information received and, as a consequence, your anxiety, borne out of ignorance about 'the reality' of your clients and their situation, may be high, perhaps unnecessarily so. This can affect the emotional tone of your personal level inter-action and lead to later significant departures. This may result particularly if you accept referrals over the telephone (see below). However, referrals from professionals, including close colleagues, may not reveal important negative or potentially complicating aspects which should be made known to you, as with Malcolm's referral from the family doctor to the Health Centre's resident counsellor. If you feel anxious or negative about a referral, it is important to try to understand from where these feelings derive, especially when they arise before you have met your clients, as with Barbara and her sadistically violent and abused young woman.

The referral may be made by a member of your clients' social network. This may be entirely appropriate and also yield relevant background information which you can use. As with referrals from colleagues, however, the information presented may be prejudiced by the nature of the relationship between referrers and clients, as well as between referrers and yourself, including what you represent for them. Some referrals are more motivated by issues concerning power and domination than genuine caring for the client.

Sheila's brother, although worried about his sister's health, had been very reluctant to return home to live with his family. It meant giving up a well-paid job which he enjoyed and losing much of his hard-won independence from the family. Consequently, he felt as if his mother had some-how 'won' and he had 'lost' in a power struggle. Bringing his sister to her initial appointment appeared altruistic but was part of his largely unarticulated wish to regain his former independent position. If he could hand over responsibility for Sheila's care entirely to a professional, he could, once again, be free.

Referral mode

If you manage your first contact with clients or their referrers in a methodical way, you will more easily discern when your usual practice is being compromised or your transaction is departing from the straightforward. Thus, if you decide that you only accept written referrals and colleagues insist on telephoning you and fail to send a written report, this may tell you something about your relationship with your colleagues, your colleagues' relationship with your potential clients or about the clients themselves. Any of these aspects may be of relevance in predicting later significant departures.

The route by which you hear about a potential referral initially influences how and what you learn about your clients prior to any subsequent interview you may offer. A verbal contact (face-to-face or via the telephone) makes it more likely that you will obtain important and sometimes relevant but subtle information about the clients. Although you may get a better overall impression of them, this may lack important factual information. This is one disadvantage of accepting self-referrals over the telephone. Therefore, it is wise to be cautious in so doing, especially if you are a single-handed practitioner, working from home, or working with a forensic client group. You may thus wish to inform your clients that you require some written referral information from others who know them, prior to offering an actual appointment. Such a response may disappoint your clients. You therefore need to be prepared for this eventuality. If you are not able to gain sufficient co-operation and collaboration in negotiating such a referral issue, this does not augur well for working together towards agreed transaction goals. It is unlikely, however, that such intolerance or upset would apply to many clients (unless you specialize in 'difficult clients'). In not laying yourself open to offering counselling to all potential clients you are not only protecting yourself but modelling, for your clients, appropriate limit-setting.

Your next step may be to request written material, especially about your clients' social network and any current or previous involvement of other professionals, and this can become a standard part of your process of assessment. Some counsellors extend this by requiring either the referrers or the clients to complete a questionnaire which has to be returned before an assessment interview is offered. The advantage of this method is that clients may find it easier to reveal factual information in writing. However, a questionnaire can be perceived as an obstacle to referral, especially if clients are not fully literate. Even if the clients have completed a questionnaire, there is no guarantee that the information communicated is more valid than that obtained at interview, since important and relevant aspects can still be omitted. Failure to appreciate the limits of questionnaires can lead you to an unfounded confidence, arising from your belief that all relevant information has been obtained.

It is important, therefore, to establish a referral procedure which suits your particular requirements in terms of the referral source, route and mode. Having a clearly defined referral process with an understandable rationale is likely to impress and inspire confidence both in referrers and clients, as well as conferring the advantages already discussed.

Setting up the first interview

Some counsellors are happy to arrange a first assessment interview 'blind'. Knowing little about their potential clients, such counsellors rely on the bona fides of the referrers. To an extent, they also infer that the clients can meet the demands of the social role of client. As discussed in earlier chapters, the demands of the client's role may exceed the capacity of some clients. If you take on 'all-comers', it can mean that a difficult decision to say 'no' is not ultimately avoided but merely delayed. Rejecting clients after assessment may be problematic and sometimes psychologically damaging, especially if this process has fostered in your clients unrealistic expectations of acceptance which are subsequently not met.

How much background, personal information and independent corroboration of factual material about potential clients you collect is a matter of individual preference. If you are a single-handed counsellor and/or working from home or in another environment which is unsupported, you may wish to err on the side of caution and request more background than your office-based counterparts. How much you tell potential clients about yourself and your counselling style, in advance of an assessment meeting, is again a matter of personal preference, professional training and theoretical orientation. Counsellors working from home will obviously communicate much about themselves without saying a word! Regardless of your setting, however, it is useful to provide a standard amount of information both before and at assessment. This means that transactions where either more or less is demanded of, or volunteered by, you are clearly recognizable.

The question of realistic expectations, both in terms of what counselling can deliver under optimal conditions and what you expect and do not expect of your clients regarding their role behaviour, needs to be addressed. When considering clients' ability to carry out their side of the counselling transaction, you need to know whether their current psychosocial adjustment is precarious and, if so, whether there is a likelihood of it deteriorating under the frustrations and pressures of counselling. With many referrals, the clients are able to cope and are not particularly at risk of significant deterioration. However, those counsellors who deliver therapy as part of a statutory duty or as directed by the courts, where a therapeutic alliance may be particularly difficult to establish, need to pay special attention to evaluating such aspects as a matter of important routine (Meloy, 1988).

With some clients it will be important, at the outset, to specify behaviours which are not compatible with successful therapy or which will not be tolerated (see Chapter 6, page 88). If not, difficulties will arise in the transaction which could have been avoided or which would have benefited from a prior discussion of the relevant issues, for example, a client arriving for a session in a drunken state. Remember, you are interested both in behaviour during sessions and in between them, which includes immediately before or after your meetings when your clients are coming and going. This is especially pertinent when working from home.

It may be helpful to inform or remind your clients of the limits inherent to your own professional role and its requirements. You should also inform professional colleagues in your immediate environment of the possibility or likelihood, in some instances, that significant departures with some of your clients could involve them. Such communication should not, of course, breach professional confidentiality, but the support derived from other professionals appreciating something of the situation should protect both you and the therapy by minimizing the effect of others' negative attitudes or behaviour on the counselling process. In addition, you may learn important information about your clients' behaviour, immediately pre- and post-sessions. With Helen, it was only after she had had her outburst and had temporarily left therapy, that her counsellor's colleagues told him that they had noticed how, at the same time each week, a very upset young woman sat in the stairwell crying and banging her head against the wall! Such knowledge might have affected Helen's therapist's view of his own 'good work'.

> *Andrew's demanding job meant he had to travel widely and he frequently had to rearrange his therapy sessions, sometimes at short notice. On the face of it, Andrew's requests were understandable and the mechanism of re-scheduling had been discussed and agreed between him and his counsellor. Gradually, his counsellor noticed that the 'legitimate' telephone calls to arrange the timing of the sessions were occurring late in the evening and regularly included an update on how Andrew was feeling. His counsellor felt there was a risk that all the counselling would soon be carried out by telephone and late at night. He considered the telephone calls to be his client's testing of the limits of the counselling transaction and of his own willingness to make himself available to Andrew. This view gained further support when, after his counsellor told Andrew that they had reached the end of a particular session, Andrew volunteered that a session 'over supper in a local restaurant' might fit in better with his own hectic schedule!*

How much you tell your clients about yourself is a matter of personal preference and theoretical orientation. Once you have established what you feel is a reasonable amount of information, however, systematically conveying this should be part of your standard 'method', regardless of whether you do this verbally or by handwritten or typed letter. Keeping to a standard format allows you to identify those clients who deviate by asking for or insisting upon more than your usual. This does not put those clients in the wrong, but it provides you with information about them which is often therapeutically relevant in terms of later significant departures.

Untoward events, involvement of others and confidentiality

It is better to anticipate untoward events, such as suicide attempts, violence or drugs and alcohol misuse, rather than to stumble upon them because you have closed your mind to those possibilities. Especially where such events are part of your clients' histories or their presenting problems, it is prudent to raise them on to the public level agenda early. You should also discuss your likely short-term response to these events and its rationale, together with any longer-term consequences which will follow. Again, these issues may be especially relevant to single-handed counsellors and those working from home.

One consequent measure may be the need to involve others, usually other professionals, in the immediate management of a crisis. Often the other professionals are the clients' family doctors and together you will need to discuss the degree to which you are free to divulge confidential information, as well as how your clients' emergency situation will be managed. You need to decide how permeable are your boundaries governing confidentiality, bearing in mind that levels of confidentiality are fluid and may be lowered if demanded by the seriousness of your clients' situation, especially if this includes threats of violence (including sexual abuse) or actual violence (see also Chapters 3 and 8).

Where other professionals are involved in providing a thera-peutic input, for example, doctors who are prescribing psycho-tropic medication for your clients' psychiatric condition, some agreed means of communication needs to be established which is clear to all concerned. Both the criteria for discussing information and the type of information to be exchanged should be decided. Without prior agreement, mutual mistrust can develop at the personal level, which undermines the public level interaction and can complicate the overall transaction.

Quality of external support
Accurately determining the nature and quality of your clients' psychosocial networks or family systems may be difficult. Your clients' impoverished or contradictory account about both the configuration and quality of support offered externally may leave you uncertain or ignorant, despite your attempts at clarification (see Chapter 4). As a result, you may choose to reject clients if

there seems little possibility of a successful outcome, or a significant chance that the clients may deteriorate, especially if there are other contra-indications, including strong predictors of likely complicating or other risk factors. In other situations, however, the assessment scales may appear evenly balanced between indications and contra-indications. Under such circumstances the nature and quality of your clients' external psychosocial support may be a crucial element in deciding whether to accept them into counselling.

> *At assessment, Barbara found her client was articulate. She remained concerned, however, by the extent of her clients' violence. She was persuaded to offer therapy having discussed her concerns with the referring psychiatrist who was willing to remain in regular, two-monthly, out-patient contact with their shared client, throughout her counselling. The psychiatrist also told Barbara that the staff at the hostel where the client lived were extremely supportive and that there was regular contact between them and the Community Mental Health Team of which the psychiatrist was a part. Considering these to be positive aspects of her clients' social network tipped the balance in favour of Barbara offering her counselling.*

Depending on the situation, you may choose to discuss with your clients your concerns about offering them counselling, together with your proposals for tackling any particular difficulty. As a result, you may propose a discussion with their doctors or other involved professionals. If so, you will need to ask their consent. In fact, talking things over with your clients may help you form a more accurate overall picture of their available psychosocial support and you may then find it easier to make an appropriate decision to accept or not. Like Barbara, you may discuss the matter with the referrers or you may seek out a suitable colleague with whom to do so. Alternatively, or in addition, you may decide to interview members of your clients' families and/or professionals already involved in your clients' care. These interviews may be either with or without your clients being present. The former has the advantage of allowing you to see and assess the nature and quality of your clients' interactions with others.

For some counsellors, interviewing other people from the clients' wider network forms a standard part of the assessment. In

Table 5.1 *Indications for brief counselling*

Your client is required to:
1 have a presenting problem which is circumscribed and provides a clear aim for brief counselling;
2 prioritize their difficulties;
3 have a presenting problem which can be formulated into a theme to provide the focus of the work;
4 have the motivation and flexibility to work towards the focus within a short time;
5 respond at assessment to a 'trial' intervention related to the focus.

As counsellor you are required to:
6 formulate and assess the suitability of the focus for brief work, e.g., a separation conflict or abnormal bereavement reaction;
7 have considered possible contra-indications to brief work and, if present, assessed whether they can be overcome or avoided.

most instances, however, it is reserved for those situations where an opinion about the quality of the clients' psychosocial network is crucial, either because it yields information necessary to help you decide whether to accept or reject the clients or because the quality of the support is itself thought to be the crucial factor in maintaining a straightforward counselling transaction and predicting a successful outcome.

Overall, it is the particular combination of features of your clients, yourself and your own setting which dictate who you receive into counselling. As part of this, however, you need to take account of not only the inherent risks *during* formal counselling but also those which pertain *between* sessions.

Limited sessions or open-ended

Tables 5.1 and 5.2 outline the main indications and contra-indications for brief counselling. In general terms, the absence of indications for brief counselling may suggest a consideration of longer-term work, although this assumes that overall, the indications for any therapy outweigh the contra-indications. Often, long-term work can result from a failure to terminate shorter-term work on time (an example of a complicated counselling transaction) or from an incomplete assessment which failed to detect potentially complicating factors which would have contra-indicated brief work but indicated long-term work. (See Hobbs, 1996 for a fuller discussion.)

Table 5.2 *General and relative contra-indications for brief counselling*

General contra-indications
A client who:
1 has a psychotic or severe depressive illness;
2 has gross destructive or self-destructive behaviour or severe somatizing disorder;
3 has a personality disorder, especially if it involves impulsive behaviour or serious substance misuse;
4 has relationships characterized by excessive dependency that may result in dependency on the counsellor which could not be successfully addressed in the time.

Relative contra-indications
A client who:
5 fails to make positive emotional contact at assessment;
6 has no feasible focus;
7 responds negatively to a 'trial' intervention;
8 has no available social support.

The indications and contra-indications for group or family therapy approaches are listed in Tables 5.3, 5.4 and 5.5. Sometimes group or family therapy approaches are tried as interventions of last resort, after complications have arisen in the individual counselling setting, and not as initial, viable therapeutic approaches in their own right (Bentovim, 1996; Bloch and Aveline, 1996; and Lask, 1987). Ideally, you will evaluate the appropriateness of these interventions during your initial assessment (see Palmer and MacMahon, 1997).

Other practical points

Behind the scenes
There are some practical aspects about setting up counselling which, although important, normally remain invisible to your clients. They are not negotiable and are not usually relevant for your clients to know in detail. They centre on your competence to deliver counselling or therapy, your affiliations to professional bodies related to or governing your profession, 'protection' in the form of insurance against any negligence claim or other professional irregularity. These requirements differ markedly from counsellor to counsellor so the subject will not be considered in further detail here. However, it is worth bearing in mind that clients may have histories of taking litigious action, which can be repeated

Table 5.3 *Indications and contra-indications for explorative group psychotherapy*

Group psychotherapy may prove useful:

1 where the predominant problems are interpersonal rather than intrapersonal, e.g., difficulty in initiating or sustaining relationships;

2 where the person is willing to participate in a group setting;

3 where the person has sufficient trust to discuss problems in a group setting and allows them to be examined constructively;

4 where there is a degree of behavioural disturbance such as violence which cannot be contained in individual work.

Group psychotherapy may be contra-indicated:

5 where there has been pronounced early and sustained deprivation, since the person may experience a group as another depriving experience in having to share the therapist;

6 if the person is extremely socially isolated and needs individual help to begin to communicate;

7 for people in acute crisis who may be too fragile;

8 for people with a diagnosis of severe depression or psychosis, severe personality disorder, brain damage or substance abuse. (The particular difficulties associated with these conditions decrease the chances of the person benefiting from the group.)

in their involvement with you. Also, any counselling transaction puts you potentially at risk of being sued, thus the issue of insurance is of direct relevance to all counsellors, even if the means to acquire it differ.

Other practical considerations are how you choose to keep a record of your clients' details and your therapeutic work together. Some professions or organizations to which you belong impose statutory duties upon you in relation to this aspect. You therefore need to be aware of these, as well as of the relevant parts of any 'data protection' legislation, especially if you make use of computerized stores or records for your casenotes.

There are also aspects regarding your personal security which relate to your workplace (especially if this is in your own home) and to other colleagues, both clinical and administrative. You need to monitor the quality of your relationships with such colleagues as well as establishing and maintaining effective communication channels. This is especially important when you have clients with whom you anticipate complications which could 'overspill' into your surrounding environment. You need to establish a work setting and working routine in which you feel physically safe and which also provides you with the necessary emotional and

Table 5.4 *Indications for family therapy (adapted from Lask, 1987)*

In general, family therapy is indicated where problems both arise from family behaviour patterns and are affected by them. Such problems are diverse but include families:

1 where there is an inability to resolve conflicts, make decisions or solve problems;
2 where there is poor organization, either too rigid or too chaotic;
3 where there is pronounced overcloseness or distance between family members;
4 where there is poor communication;
5 where there is parental failure to work together, to the detriment of the children;
6 where transgenerational alliances are interfering with the family functioning, e.g., grandparents and children against parents.

In child and adolescent settings family therapy is useful for families:

7 where physical disorders are present in which psychological factors are involved in causing or aggravating the problem, e.g., diabetes, asthma, anorexia nervosa;
8 where there are physical disorders with adverse psychological sequelae, e.g., cystic fibrosis, malignant disease, chronic renal disease;
9 where there are behavioural and emotional problems such as school refusal, phobias, difficult or defiant behaviour;
10 where there is child abuse or neglect (see contra-indications).

In adult settings indications for family therapy include:

11 relationship problems;
12 family tension;
13 recurrent or chronic ill health;
14 poor adjustment to changes in the family life cycle such as bereavement, children leaving home or an elderly grandparent coming to live with the family.

Table 5.5 *Contra-indications for family therapy*

Contra-indications for family therapy are where:

1 a family does not want help;
2 violence or sexual abuse have occurred and a child is unlikely to express feelings in the presence of the perpetrator. (However, a family approach may be used later if rehabilitation of the child and parents is contemplated.)

intellectual support via appropriate supervision of your work. This applies regardless of your level of seniority and experience.

You need to identify professionals who agree to provide second opinions and acquaint yourself with alternative therapeutic resources in case your clients require these in the event of counselling breaking down or their mental state deteriorating seriously (see Chapter 8). In the most complicated of counselling transactions, just knowing that professional supports are in place can help you to maintain some clients effectively in counselling. These external resources can also minimize any psychological damage caused by unsuccessful counselling. Appropriately managing transfers from you to another therapist or agency can mean that re-referral to you remains a future possibility and disruption of therapy is kept to an absolute minimum. Many professionals are willing to provide support to you in a crisis, especially if they have been warned in advance that their input might be required.

Attendance and breaks
You will need to stress the importance of regular and punctual attendance and agree a mechanism via which you can contact your clients, and vice versa, in the event of unexpected breaks. Holidays and other planned breaks need to be discussed in 'business' terms, for example, how much notice is given, if usual fees (where applicable) are charged and if replacement sessions are offered. Ideally, all of this is agreed at the outset.

It is good practice to open any discussion about other practical or business aspects early on, for example, the anticipated duration of counselling or the potential need to involve others in the assessment and therapeutic process. You may also consider whether you discuss the possibility of marital, family or group therapy as part of your initial assessment or introductory discussion. Stressing to your clients, at the beginning of counselling, any anticipated difficulties with the ending of the transaction is also of crucial importance. Emphasizing how the counselling relationship differs from friendship may be important. Unlike a friendship, with counselling, the closer and more meaningful the relationship becomes the nearer it is to reaching its ending. Viewed in this light, it can be seen how different an ordinary personal relationship is from the counselling transaction, with its additional, yet intrinsic, public level.

What to tell and what not to tell
It is not possible at the beginning of counselling to anticipate and plan your response to all eventualities, nor would this necessarily be desirable. After all, as counsellor, your prime role is to be receptive to the appropriate needs of your clients, that is to facilitate the expression of their concerns and formulate their predicaments. You need to strike a balance, therefore, between providing them with sufficient information and swamping them through introducing too much, too soon, thereby increasing the

risk of overloading the public level agenda and complicating the overall transaction.

Your professional experience and judgement, based on your own particular circumstances, will dictate what and how much you say. As a general rule, less is better, especially as at this early stage you do not understand much about your clients' styles of relating. In some situations, however, where the likelihood of significant departures is high, it may be that the bare minimum is substantial and there may even be times when an explicit therapy contract is required (see Chapter 6). Of course, sometimes your clients will experience your bare minimum as 'too much'.

The overriding aim at the beginning of counselling is to foster your clients' capacity to fulfil their role as effectively as possible. This aim should inform your interventions and alert you to the fact that some clients will require more education and support than others to achieve it. You need to provide these elements, mindful of engendering false hopes or expectations or encouraging undue dependency or pessimism.

Saying 'no'
No matter how skilful and experienced you are, or how well supported in your professional environment, you will turn away some clients. You may feel a variety of emotions in response: guilt, shame, depression, anxiety, relief or even exhilaration. Ideally, you will reject the clients for understandable reasons, at least some of which you will have discussed with them. Sometimes, however, you may not have clearly thought out reasons, despite discussing the situation with colleagues, supervisors or the referrers. Under such circumstances, you have been persuaded by your 'gut reaction' or intuition. As one counsellor commented, contact with a particular client 'made the hairs on the back of my neck stand on end'. Such physiological responses should not be ignored!

If declining to take on clients, you need to inform them without increasing the psychological pain and disappointment inherent in your news. Very occasionally, the rejection will be received gratefully. In these circumstances, the assessment itself may have achieved some limited benefit, even if the presenting problems remain largely unsolved. For some clients, the news of rejection may be perceived within their sado-masochistic psychological framework and become perversely enjoyable. They then feel 'better' for being rejected because this fits with an inner belief about their selves as being bad and in need of punishment. Peter's client, for example, told him, with a gleeful look on his face, that he had been 'rejected' by two previous therapists after their assessment interviews. Perhaps this should have alerted Peter to future difficulties during his assessment, although these soon became evident.

If you have made it clear to your clients, from the outset, that there is a possibility of not taking them on for therapy, you will be less pressurized to rationalize or excuse your decision defensively. The more you can discuss the reasons for your decision with your clients, in language which is accessible and in a tone which is non-judgemental and non-blaming, the more the termination phase should be straightforward. Any termination, however, is likely to involve some pain for you and your clients, and you should ensure that you have allocated enough time to do justice to this important and delicate task.

It may be helpful to describe to your clients why you thought counselling was not appropriate. This can often be made more meaningful if you refer to positive aspects as well as to specific parts of your assessment where you felt the transaction was untenable. Providing your clients with this food for thought may help them, in the future, to re-approach counselling in a more thoughtful way. Obviously, if you feel that some aspects which you tried to explore in your assessment have reached a stalemate and are not open to further thought or re-evaluation, there is little to be gained by your clients in discussing them further. Some clients will be bitterly disappointed at your 'rejection' of them and will convey their feelings in the form of anger and verbal aggression. Clearly, actual physical violence is also a possible reaction which should be borne in mind, especially with clients who have a history of violence either as victims or as perpetrators.

Endings

As already mentioned, endings should be borne in mind from the beginning of the referral process. Your assessment must involve a consideration of the likely benefits of counselling and the extent to which further help might be required, even after the end of a fruitful counselling transaction. Indeed, if you anticipate that the future necessary resources are not available, this might be a strong contra-indication for ever starting therapy. You will also need to consider the action you might be required to take if the counselling transaction breaks down or ends prematurely, for whatever reason. In addition, you need to assess the likely psychological impact on the clients of the ending of therapy.

Where it is agreed that therapy is time-limited, ending tends to become an automatic focus and occupy a prominent position in both your minds. However, this is not necessarily the case. On the basis of their past experience, endings will be problematic for many of your clients and, in some instances, the amount of ambivalence and associated avoidance of emotional pain is extremely high. The onus is therefore on you to remember the end date and help your clients face the psychological work required so that separation and loss can be successfully negotiated without this process becoming more traumatic than it is therapeutic.

Where no arrangement to terminate has been agreed at the outset, you will need to consider carefully the benefits of continuing treatment on an open-ended basis against the debits of fostering undue dependence or simply marking time, that is continuing counselling without obvious beneficial results. In practice, it is often difficult to differentiate between a potentially creative 'fallow' period (Khan, 1983) and that of sterile and rote attendance.

The crucial requirement is that you provide a realistic amount of time for your clients to achieve the necessary psychological accomplishments which support the ending of your counselling transaction. This will vary from client to client. While the main responsibility for concluding therapy rests with you, optimally, its precise timing becomes part of the public level agenda and is discussed by both of you, as far as possible on an equal footing.

Summary

There may be early indications in your counselling transactions of later significant departures. Sometimes these indications may be apparent even before you meet your clients. Appreciating these can help you think about and organize practical aspects of your therapeutic work. These aspects can then help rather than hinder the detection and correction of potentially complicating influences which may reside in you, your clients or your respective psycho-social networks.

It is better to anticipate significant departures since 'prevention is better than cure'. Hence, you need to have a strategy for accepting referred clients which you state clearly to both referrers and clients. Your referral process should also stipulate acceptable routes, sources and modes of referral.

Your clients will vary according to the amount and type of support they require to perform their role of client adequately. Consequently, you will respond to them differentially according to their needs. Careful evaluation of their problems, psychological strengths and coping ability will inform your interventions, especially where there is a need to involve others in their immediate or long-term management. Early on you need to assess the quality and degree of support in your clients' wider psychosocial networks. You need to monitor any changes in these networks or in the counselling transaction's requirement of them, otherwise the effect of changes can compromise the straightforwardness of your transaction.

Even with the most elaborate of assessment protocols and effective inter-professional communication networks, counselling transactions end prematurely and painfully for reasons which are not foreseeable. Hence, it is important to keep endings in mind from the start. Only by doing so is it likely that the termination phase of the transaction will be therapeutic rather than simply traumatizing.

6

Preserving Respective Roles

An important aim of your interventions is to maintain the straight-forward character of the counselling transaction or to return a complicated transaction to the straightforward. How you intervene, however, depends upon how you conceive the departures and complications. Your thinking will be importantly influenced by whether or not your public–personal equilibrium has shifted significantly. You therefore need to evaluate this before proceeding to intervene at all (see Chapter 7).

Having established that your public–personal equilibrium is within its normal limits, you are in a position to decide how to construe the observed departure or complication. Sometimes you will consider it to be limited to one or other levels of interaction within the overall transaction, public or personal. At other times, both levels may be thought to be involved. Regardless, there is a range of interventions which you can deploy aimed at preserving yours and your clients' respective roles (see Figure 6.1).

However, you need to be aware that your interventions may produce departures or complications. Therefore you should continually re-assess your own public–personal equilibrium. This is part of your ongoing work of monitoring the whole counselling transaction. Where your public–personal equilibrium becomes significantly disturbed, your approach to intervening will need to differ (see Chapter 7).

Interventions

There are a number of interventions for dealing with departures from the straightforward counselling transaction. These centre on

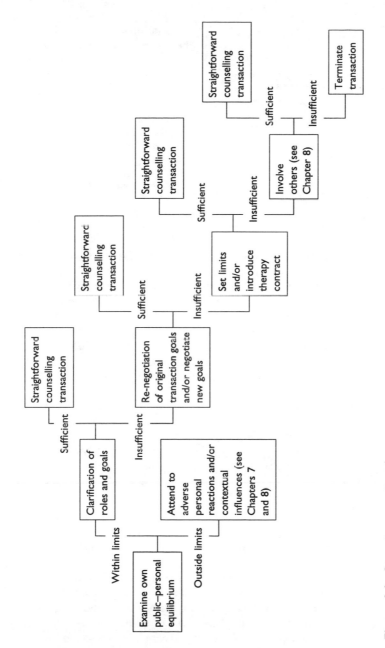

Figure 6.1 *Preserving respective roles*

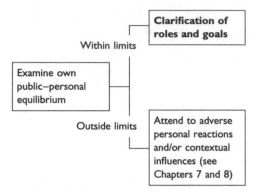

Figure 6.2　*Clarification of roles and goals*

clarifying the previously agreed transaction goals and aspects of the roles required of you and your clients, so that the goals may be conscientiously pursued. These interventions require your educational and negotiating skills as well as your ability to set limits and a determination to stand firm, if necessary. Where departures have developed into complications (that is significant departures), and attempts to rectify them have failed, you may need to intervene to terminate the transaction or to arrange for the transfer of your clients to another therapist, agency or even institution, such as psychiatric hospital, at least for a time. These various interventions are also discussed below.

Clarification of roles and goals
Your clients will not necessarily know how to fulfil their role as clients or what to expect from you as a professional. Thus, you may need to educate them about even seemingly obvious behaviour expected of a client, such as regular and punctual attendance (see Figure 6.2). Andrew, for example, although a professional business-man, well-used to taking the initiative at work, did not appreciate the commitment his therapy would require and he needed to be informed and repeatedly reminded of this by his counsellor.

With some clients, it may be useful to indicate how your role as counsellor differs from those of other professionals, such as a General Practitioner or Health Visitor, with whom your clients are already familiar. You might wish to compare and contrast the different sets of skills involved. It may be useful to emphasize the differences between the conventional and somewhat passive 'patient' role and the more active role expected of a client in counselling. In this way, you help to establish a mutual and reciprocal set of expectations which are consonant with your respective roles. Later, when any departures or complications arise, you are able to remind your clients of your earlier discussions and understandings.

Clients often struggle to accept even the basic level of responsibility, often feeling that merely attending their sessions should be sufficient. Ownership of emotional responsibility for their presenting problems, especially where this involves anti-social or other maladaptive behaviour, is often problematic. Barbara found this with her client but was eventually able to help her realize that even though she was responsible, as the perpetrator, for specific past violent events, Barbara would not sit in judgement over her on account of these.

In the above instance, Barbara stressed that her role was to understand what motivated her clients' abusive and violent behaviour and how this had left the latter feeling afterwards. She found that explaining differences between her role as counsellor and that of professionals working in the penal system, with whom her client had previously come into repeated contact, was time-consuming but worthwhile. In fact, it took many months before her client began to understand Barbara's position and the implications of her professional role. This coincided with her client's capacity to acknowledge more fully responsibility for her own anti-social behaviour.

Sometimes the goal of the transaction is not clear. This may be because your clients have failed to voice an obvious problem or complaint. If so, you need to find out whether there are any major unresolved issues in your clients' lives, such as earlier bereavements, traumatic separations, domestic violence, sexual abuse, or the secondary effects of addiction, which are actually problematic. In other transactions, after the presenting problem has been resolved, your clients may want to continue counselling. Under these circumstances you need to clarify why they wish to keep attending and try to identify any hidden additional, but still relevant, goals for the counselling transaction. You may need to state clearly the complaints which are relevant, as well as specifying those problems with which you are qualified to help. Your professional context and training will obviously exert strong influences.

When your clients present with multiple problems, you may need to help them decide which to concentrate on, especially if counselling time is limited. As part of this task, you may establish that some problems are inter-linked and can be addressed together as a single composite focus. These discussions often require personal information that your clients have not previously volunteered. As Peter found out (page 55), you may meet resistance to such personal disclosure. If so, it is important to explain clearly why you require particular information and how this can help you to help your clients. Otherwise, if your clients are unaware of your need to know particular details, they may be reluctant to tell you. In addition, your clients may misinterpret your curiosity about a topic as a sign of your personal intrusiveness rather than professional interest. In order to maintain the straightforward character of the counselling transaction it is important to avoid such misunderstandings.

Your clients may be prevented from disclosing personal information by a basic mistrust in professionals, by low self-esteem or ambivalence about seeking help (see page 16). You may find it useful to explain the importance of establishing an open dialogue, while indicating that you appreciate the reasons for their reticence and how mistrust, low self-esteem and ambivalence pose very real obstacles to their establishing a therapeutic alliance with you. You need to explain that their personal information will help you form a more complete picture of them in their wider psychosocial and historical context.

Such explanations may not help, since, especially at the beginning of counselling, some clients easily feel patronized. When this is so, you will have merely reinforced the mistrust, low self-esteem or ambivalence. It is important, therefore, to avoid 'lectures', which would hopefully be a departure from your own straightforward style, but stress that developing an appropriate degree of mutual trust within the counselling transaction inevitably takes time. You may also wish to convey that some aspects of your clients' obstructive interpersonal attitudes were, historically, a matter of self-preservation. To a certain extent these protected them against their earlier experiences of abusive or neglectful individuals who were in positions of power and authority over them. You need to emphasize to your clients, however, that maintaining these maladaptive styles of relating impoverishes their current relationships.

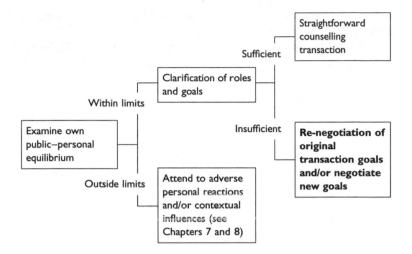

Figure 6.3 *Re-negotiation of goals*

Malcolm's counsellor spent most of two therapy sessions trying to establish clearly the nature of her client's daytime problem. Malcolm had been reluctant to disclose this, being embarrassed and ashamed to admit to thoughts, feelings and behaviour which he and his partner regarded as infantile (see page 46). He revealed them only after his counsellor repeatedly assured him that embarrassment and shame were often associated with personal disclosure and were to be expected. He was surprised at the relief he then felt at being able to speak openly about his 'tantrums' but in a serious and mature fashion. An exploration of the antecedents of his 'tantrums' became one of the therapeutic goals of the transaction.

Re-negotiation of goals

Sometimes, as we saw with Malcolm (page 4), the reiteration or re-definition of the original transaction goals is sufficient to return the transaction to the straightforward, at least for a while. At other times, however, this intervention is ineffective and the next step is to consider re-negotiating the original goals (see Figure 6.3). This may include the removal of some or the introduction of other new goals to the public level agenda. In this way, previously neglected or minor goals, which have assumed a greater and genuine importance, can be justifiably included as goals of the overall transaction. Adjusting the public level agenda may be sufficient to return the transaction to the straightforward, as in the following example.

> *Sheila's counsellor initially focused on her clients' presented eating disorder. In fact, the counsellor arranged with Sheila that she was weighed regularly and that they both knew her weight at the start of each session. In spite of, or because of this, most of the sessions centred on issues concerning Sheila's diet and calorie intake. This continued even after Sheila's weight increased to within normal limits for her age and height. It was only when Sheila told her counsellor about the termination of her pregnancy that she realized how little she knew of Sheila's lifestyle and wider relationships. The only hint that Sheila gave was when she mentioned her brother's annoyance at 'having' to return home. Picking up this cue, Sheila's counsellor suggested that 'emotional blackmail' might form part of the family's regulatory mechanism for staying intact. Sheila readily agreed, volunteering that she felt manipulated and controlled by this style of interaction which was used by both her mother and brother. She added that she suspected that she also used such 'power tactics'. She believed that a direct expression of her needs would inevitably upset her family. It was decided that the family's power relationships would become a topic for discussion with the agreed goal of trying to change Sheila's part in them.*

Following this discussion and re-negotiation of goals, the counselling transaction progressed and Sheila's preoccupation with eating disappeared from the public level agenda. Sheila's counsellor suspected the initial goals concerning the eating disorder might have been used to test her, before she could be entrusted with these deeper concerns but she kept this speculation to herself.

Limit-setting and therapy contracts

In the process of clarifying your respective roles and re-negotiating new goals, you may conclude that the original goals are still the most important. You thus decide that the originally negotiated goals remain appropriate but that you need to support the integrity of the public level interaction by setting limits to what can realistically be tolerated in terms of clients' role behaviour within the transaction (see Figure 6.4). You may need to specify the limits to which you are able or prepared to go in order to try to help your clients. Sometimes, it can be useful to reinforce this limit-setting by drawing up a therapy contract.

> *The counselling transaction between Peter and his client departed from the straightforward very early on (see page 2). Even though Peter acknowledged to himself that he had not been as meticulous as usual in explaining his method of working, in particular, the reasons for his note-taking, he felt that this was an insufficient departure to account entirely for his clients' aberrant and unacceptable behaviour at interview. (Peter was so affected by it that he felt he might be unable to work with this client.) Reluctant to be so negative so early, however, Peter had decided to try to keep an open mind and observe whether his client would eventually conform, more conventionally, to his clients' role. When this proved not to be the case, Peter suggested that they agreed some 'ground rules' (Peter's phrase for a 'therapy contract') for their future encounters.*
>
> *Peter's client was initially confused and suspicious of his counsellor's motives when he proposed a discussion about their mutual expectations. Gradually, however, he realized that Peter took notice of what he said and although he prevaricated, he eventually agreed to his side of the contract. This was that he would attend punctually or else inform Peter of his anticipated absence or lateness and not attend if he had taken alcohol or drugs. For his part, Peter agreed to make it clear to his client what he was noting and tell his client if he felt so concerned about his behaviour or mental state that he needed to discuss the situation with other involved professionals, namely his manager and family doctor.*

The use of even a simple therapy contract, as above, should not be considered lightly since there are many pitfalls which need to be avoided. The most common is introducing the contract when both you and your client feel hostile to one another (see Miller, 1989). A contract forged under such circumstances is unlikely to succeed. Intense hostility, which might have motivated your decision to implement the contract, needs to subside, at least to an extent. In

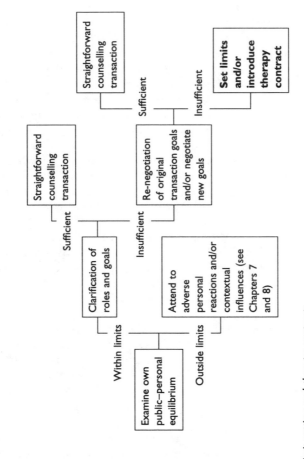

Figure 6.4 *Limit setting and therapy contracts*

other words, you must regain some of your usual public–personal equilibrium if the contract is to be satisfactorily implemented and begin to help break a stalemate and return the transaction to the straightforward.

Introducing the idea of a contract may require tact, as it may be experienced by your clients as patronizing, annoying or humiliating, particularly if they feel an unequal party in the negotiations or if you try to set more conditions than your clients can meet. Under such circumstances, the contract is likely to break down, even if there is initial agreement. Peter's client struggled to keep to the negotiated therapy contract but it became clear that remaining sober was highly problematic. Peter referred him to his local drugs and alcohol misuse team who were happy to provide informal support between his counselling sessions. This extra therapeutic input seemed to help, at least for a time.

If the contractual conditions require your clients to give up their only strategies (for example, illicit drugs and alcohol) for coping with intolerable feelings and if no viable alternative coping strategy is offered or is available to them, the contract is unlikely to succeed. It is therefore imperative that any contractual conditions are realistic (Sills, 1997). Accurate empathy with your clients' situation is often required to develop a workable contract. Achieving this is a considerable undertaking, since it is often a breakdown in the therapeutic alliance and rapport which has led you to use a limit-setting contract in the first place.

Other professionals involved with your clients need to know of any implications of your contract for their own therapeutic approaches (see below, p. 96). Sometimes a therapy contract may inadvertently conflict with the requirements or conditions of another approach. Clearly this situation is one to be avoided but it can often arise when professionals are ignorant of either the presence or nature of each other's input.

With Peter's client, the situation became complex because of the multi-agency involvement, namely, the family doctor and members of the drugs and alcohol service counselling team. One of the confusing aspects for Peter's client was that all the professionals, except his probation officer counsellor, agreed to see him whether or not he was sober. Peter's client thus felt that Peter was being obstructive and unsympathetic in declaring that sessions were 'off limits' when he had been

*drinking, and he threatened to stop his counselling rather
than comply with the conditions Peter had laid down.*

*Realizing how significant the apparent inconsistency of the
differing professional approaches was, Peter discussed with
his client the need to call a meeting of all the involved professionals. Peter volunteered to both convene and chair this
meeting which, to his surprise, all agreed to attend. He
decided to conduct the meeting in two parts. First, he would
meet with all the professionals together. Secondly, they would
all meet together with their mutual client, but only after they
had agreed on a strategy.*

*At the first meeting it became clear that, while the family
doctor had understood Peter's insistence that his client
attended sessions sober, the drugs and alcohol team had not.
They felt that Peter's expectation of his client was unreasonably high as they were used to dealing with, and had the
resources to cope with, the problems associated with a clients'
acute intoxication. They were unsympathetic to those, such as
Peter, whom they thought wished to avoid these difficulties.*

*During the discussion, Peter emphasized that a consistent
stance, in both attitude and behaviour, was required from the
professionals concerned if their mutual client was to have a
chance of experiencing a consistent delivery of therapy.
Eventually, all saw the sense of this point. When their client
joined the second meeting he was informed of the discussion,
the previous professional misunderstanding and its resolution, which was that this negotiated approach would be
maintained and pursued by all concerned. It was also agreed
that there would be regular review meetings of all relevant
professionals, together with Peter's client, to monitor how far
the new agreements made were being adhered to.*

Involving others

You may have progressed through examining and re-examining
your personal and contextual influences, re-defining the original
transaction goals or negotiating new goals, to the implementation
of a therapy contract, only to discover that the counselling transaction remains essentially complicated. In part, this state of affairs
testifies to the greater stability of the complicated counselling
transaction compared to that of the straightforward (see Chapter 2,
page 25). Sometimes your efforts to return the transaction to the

straightforward have been appreciated by your clients and there will have been no further deterioration at the personal level of your interaction. At other times, repeated failure to rectify the situation has worsened your interpersonal interaction, further eroding any remaining mutual trust and respect. It is quite possible, therefore, that by the time you have failed to resolve a difficulty via the use of a therapy contract, the therapeutic alliance which binds you and your clients together is fragile and tenuous. How to proceed, therefore, calls for thought and planning rather than precipitate action. It may be that your counselling transaction is close to its end, even if many of its original goals remain unachieved.

At this point, if you have not done so already, you might consider involving others in the transaction (see Figure 6.5). If you do, you should consider whether to directly involve other professionals, who may already be involved indirectly, or to involve other members of your clients' wider psychosocial network. The circumstances of your particular transaction will dictate which members you seek to include and whether their involvement is in the short term or long term. A short-term involvement might be used solely to shed light on the current situation. Long-term involvement might entail the integration of treatment approaches so that the input of outside professionals is harnessed to your own, resulting in a coherent therapeutic strategy. Sometimes this can be accomplished by working with another professional as a cotherapist. Alternatively, it may mean a change of focus from individual to family or couple work. (Chapter 8 deals with these aspects in more detail.)

Moving from individual to family or couple therapy may be outside your professional range. If so, you may need to review your skills and training and either consider increasing the amount or type of your supervision or obtaining further professional training. If these options are not available you may need to refer your clients to another therapist who has the requisite skills.

Terminating therapy

Even if you feel you have nothing further to offer your clients, or their families or partners, it is important that you consider the possibility of referral to another counsellor or therapist. Another professional may regard your 'difficult client' as simply challenging or complex. In the face of what you perceive to be therapeutic failure, it can be difficult to remain objective (that is retain your

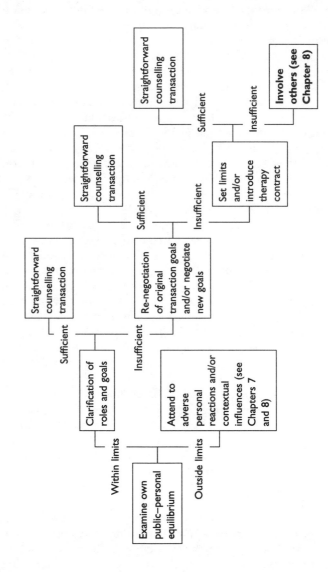

Figure 6.5 *Involving others*

usual public–personal equilibrium) and to decide what is truly in the interests of your clients.

Sometimes it is appropriate for you to terminate counselling without referring clients elsewhere (see Figure 6.6). Where transfer or termination appear to be the only viable options, you will need to ensure that the change does not cause your clients undue emotional upset. In such circumstances, it is unlikely that there will be 'no hard feelings'. In most instances, therefore, your aim is to avoid making matters worse. When termination is at the top of the public level agenda, it can be helpful to set a date, in the not too distant future, to work towards. With some transactions the urgency of the clinical situation or the degree to which the personal level interaction has deteriorated will mean this date is non-negotiable. In other transactions, unsuccessful therapy means that statutory duties come into operation which govern your subsequent management and may include compulsory treatment and incarceration. You need to be keenly aware of the constraints imposed on you by any of your wider professional obligations.

Summary

Some departures from the straightforward counselling transaction which may become established as complications arise without upsetting your public–personal equilibrium beyond its usual limits. In these situations you should be free to, thoughtfully and sensitively, use a range of therapeutic interventions to try to maintain the straightforward transaction or return the complicated transaction to the straightforward. These interventions include the use of education, clarification, negotiation or re-negotiation of clinical goals, and setting limits, which may be supported by drawing up a formal contract of therapy. These interventions can usefully be deployed in a systematic fashion, with close monitoring of the transaction, to ensure that the intervention itself has not created more problems than it is attempting to solve. Monitoring includes assessing and re-assessing your own public–personal equilibrium, as only after doing this can you confidently deploy the interventions discussed in this chapter. You will be unlikely to adhere precisely to the outlined scheme of interventions in every transaction.

When the interventions described fail to maintain the straightforward transaction or return the complicated transaction to the

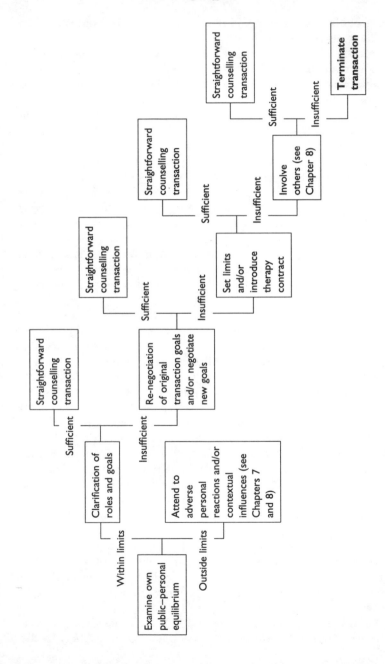

Figure 6.6 *Terminating therapy*

straightforward, it is important to re-evaluate your own personal and contextual influences. It may be that your initial appraisal of your clients was inaccurate or that, during your interventions, your public–personal equilibrium has changed significantly as a result of adverse interpersonal or contextual influences. The reason for both of these situations is likely to be that unrecognized departures are operating within the personal level interaction. These may require attention and specific interventions in their own right which go beyond that of clarification, negotiation and limit-setting.

7

Restoring the Public–Personal Equilibrium

Some counselling transactions remain complicated in spite of attempts to return them to the straightforward. You may have clarified and re-negotiated your respective roles and progressed to using therapy contracts, all to no avail. If this is the case, it is likely that the significant departures which remain are maintained by powerful emotional factors operative at the personal level of your transaction. These reflect deeply-rooted interaction patterns which may have originated in yours or your clients' past relationships. Such significant departures hamper the pursuit of public level therapeutic goals.

When faced with the failure of the interventions discussed in Chapter 6, it is important to re-evaluate your own public–personal equilibrium, since it is likely that you will be involved in an enactment of one of the three basic interaction patterns (see Chapter 2). You need to assess any alteration in your usual public–personal equilibrium to decide whether to proceed differently or intervene actively. Sometimes simply recognizing a significant shift in your usual public–personal equilibrium can bring it back to within its usual limits. This change may be sufficient to affect the whole transaction and return it to the straightforward. Where this does not occur, however, you will need to intervene actively (see Figure 7.1).

Your interventions will have two main aims which are frequently interlinked. The first is to constrain the complicating effect of the interpersonal aspects which are inappropriate to the present transaction (as with Peter's client or with Helen). The second is to allow appropriate emotions to permeate to the public level interaction (as with Sheila or Andrew). The prime objective of the

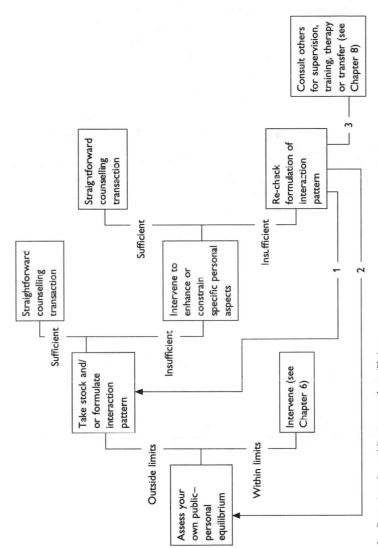

Figure 7.1 *Restoring the public–personal equilibrium*

intervention is to restore the public–personal equilibrium, via attention to public and personal level departures, to that of the straightforward counselling transaction.

How you intervene will depend upon, first, the direction in which your public–personal equilibrium has shifted, and, secondly, whether that of your client has shifted in the same or opposite direction to your own. These two pieces of information help you identify the particular basic interaction pattern. Next, you may need to find a way of raising the interpersonal issues, contributing to the basic interaction pattern, on to the public level agenda for discussion. Throughout the process, however, you need to monitor closely your own public–personal equilibrium to ensure that it returns to within your usual range for a straightforward counselling transaction. Otherwise, it may be that one basic interaction pattern is simply being substituted for another. It may help to construct a transaction window to depict your transaction, either for your own use, looking at ways of intervening to affect the two levels of interaction, or for use in supervision (Norton and Smith, 1994).

Assessing the counsellor's public–personal equilibrium

The basic interaction pattern influences how you think, feel and behave, and hence how you respond to your clients. This will vary according to the direction of equilibrium shift, whether in favour of the public or personal level. Close supervision of your counselling will enable you to recognize your experience of departures which signal a shift in the direction of public or personal dominance. The more familiar you are with the experience of such shifts themselves, the sooner you can identify them and the less their presence disturbs your professional composure. With time you are able to recognize trends in your reactions, for example to depressed or angry clients, and to notice the differing ways you respond to various types of client. Recognizing these idiosyncratic reactions and responses also allows you to note when you depart from your own norms.

Shifts towards public dominance
A shift towards public level dominance within the transaction will often feel quite different from how you feel in your usual

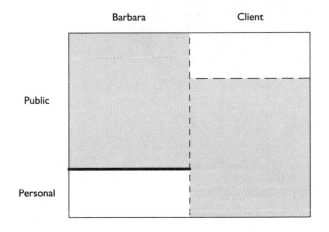

Figure 7.2a *Shifts towards public dominance*

straightforward counselling transactions. It is clear to you that you are departing from your own norms (see Figure 7.2a). Sometimes, however, the situation is less clear, even though you may be painfully aware that all is not right within the counselling transaction.

Barbara maintained a capacity to function professionally, as evidenced by her questions aimed at clarifying her client's relationship with her mother. This apparently ordinary public level work, however, was not supported by Barbara's usual personal level sensitivity and reactivity. As she realized much later, she was extremely fearful of her client. Barbara felt totally absorbed during the sessions, however, signalling her excessive public level preoccupation which lacked the usual mixture of emotional responsiveness and intellectual distance available to those of her other clients engaged in straightforward transactions. This probably accounted for her difficulty remembering the content of her sessions, the first sign she noticed of a departure from the straightforward transaction.

In her earlier career as a psychiatric nurse in a secure (locked) hospital ward, Barbara had faced many challenging and physically threatening situations. Within the culture of the hospital, any

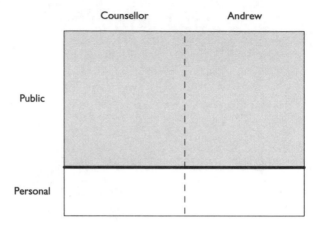

Figure 7.2b *Shifts towards public dominance*

expression by staff of their feelings in the face of professional difficulty was regarded as a sign of personal inadequacy and unprofessionalism, especially where negative emotions, such as dislike or fear of clients, were concerned. Indeed, these restrictive attitudes, which Barbara found inhumane, had impelled her to change career and also to obtain further psychodynamic training. This particular transaction shared some features with those in the secure psychiatric ward and elicited a stolid and defensive reaction from Barbara, during which it was as if her personal reaction to her client was disallowed. This style of reacting also resonated with her earlier family experiences where she learned that direct expressions of fear were viewed as a sign of vulnerability which was often exploited, especially by her elder sister. Initially, Barbara did not realize how far the public level had come to dominate, since what she was experiencing was so familiar to her.

As above, the departures from the straightforward which you need to identify can be subtle. Thus, a shift towards public level dominance and away from the personal level of the transaction may be disconcertingly similar to your usual professional style in terms of thoughts, attitudes, verbal and non-verbal behaviour. Alternatively, also making its recognition difficult, the shift towards public level dominance may occur slowly, as with Andrew's counsellor (see Figure 7.2b)

Initially, counselling Andrew had felt easy and rewarding. Andrew's counsellor was relieved that he had been referred an intelligent and articulate client with whom he identified in terms of his social background and education. It was only gradually that the counsellor realized that he frequently thought about his own social life while seeing Andrew. In particular, he noticed that he spent much of each session, when not educating Andrew about the nature and effects of anxiety and depression, deciding on his plans for the coming evening. It was not until the counsellor found that he was failing to write up sessions, which he usually did diligently, that he realized the extent of his emotional dislocation from his client. It was as if he were performing counselling 'on auto-pilot', without his usual level of intellectual and emotional engagement.

The departures, which Andrew's counsellor found so difficult to detect, largely involved *omissions*, for example, an absence of his usual sense of personal engagement with his client. You need to register such departures as potentially shedding light, not only on your public–personal equilibrium but on the basic interaction pattern in which you are involved. It is important, therefore, that you do not adopt an overly self-critical attitude to departures, registering them as anti-therapeutic mistakes or sins for which you must atone. They represent opportunities for you to think about your interaction with your clients from a different standpoint, which may help you understand the nature and style of your clients' previous influential interactions, often also prominent in their currently presented problems.

Shifts towards personal dominance

Your experience of a shift towards personal dominance may be obviously outside your norms for a straightforward counselling transaction (see Figure 7.3). This was the case with Peter (see page 2) who was in no doubt that his usual public–personal equilibrium had been upset by his clients' verbal tirade and insistence on sitting beside him.

Peter quickly noted that his equilibrium had been upset (shifting towards personal dominance) but he continued to feel anxious and angry. However, with time, his usual composure and emotional disposition returned, which

Peter   Client

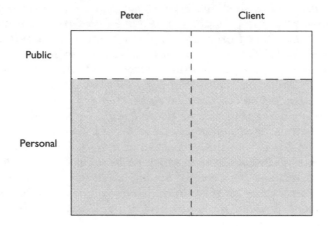

Figure 7.3 *Shifts towards personal dominance*

*allowed him to continue his assessment more effectively,
guiding it towards less emotionally charged areas of his
client's experience. Although he realized he needed to understand the reasons for his client's outburst, he decided that this
might be counter-productive during such a problematic and
complicated first interview. Peter worked to terminate the
session without further mishap, arranging another appointment for after his return from leave to explore the origins and
meaning of his client's outburst and to complete his assessment.*

As with public dominance of the public–personal equilibrium,
your experience of a shift in the personal direction may be difficult
to distinguish from that of a straightforward transaction, as the
signs of complication may be subtle. Sometimes recognizing
departures is problematic when important aspects of your own
past interactions, of which you may be only dimly aware, are re-
enacted. At other times, however, shifts are experienced as
positive, since they evoke in you a sense of job satisfaction or
personal achievement (Temple, 1996).

*When Helen returned to see her counsellor after their
unscheduled break, the latter completed his assessment of*

her. This revealed intensely ambivalent feelings towards Helen's sexually abusive father who had died five years earlier, which had not been detected previously. After discussing this topic, unresolved grief became an agreed transaction goal which they would aim to explore. This session being close to the anniversary of the death, Helen stated that she always felt suicidal around this time. She added that, although wanting to visit her father's grave, she had never had the courage to do so.

Feeling moved by his client's account, Helen's counsellor found himself offering to accompany Helen to the cemetery the following week, to give her the necessary confidence. He explained that such a visit, although likely to be emotionally painful, might help her to overcome her unresolved feelings of grief. In the event, the excursion took place as discussed. Helen was upset but remained composed throughout and her counsellor felt some satisfaction in having been able to support his client.

At the next session, however, a very different Helen appeared. She was dressed smartly with prominent use of cosmetics, which contrasted with her previously drab and untidy appearance. Helen's counsellor was surprised by this sudden transformation but, linking it to the visit to the cemetery, was content to see it as a welcomed 'improvement'. He was not prepared for what subsequently developed, however, which was her strong erotic attachment to himself. Helen attempted to turn their professional relationship into a personal friendship, if not much more.

After you have noted any significant departure from your usual professional style and emotional disposition, and determined in which direction your public–personal equilibrium has moved, you are no further forward in knowing whether the departure originates primarily in yourself or your clients. In fact, often you do not need to hastily determine its origins, since attempts to do so might well lead to further departures (Carpy, 1989). In order to decide how to proceed and whether or not to intervene, however, you do need to find out whether your clients are in an equivalent or complementary position with respect to you, that is what is the basic interaction pattern between you.

Assessing your clients' public–personal equilibrium

You can identify a shift in your clients' public–personal equilibrium either directly, by observing their verbal and non-verbal behaviour, which provides evidence of the direction of the shift, or indirectly, using your evaluation of your own equilibrium shift. Indirect identification requires you to distinguish between transactions where you and your clients have moved significantly in the same direction (both towards public or both towards personal dominance) and transactions where your's and your clients' equilibria have moved in opposite directions.

Evidence for your clients' public direction shift, however, may be difficult to identify, even when you are alert to its possibility. In part, this is because the evidence may be an absence of appropriate personal level participation, as in Andrew's case (page 27), rather than to a presence or excess of some aspect. In part, it may be because you feel overwhelmed by personal level material which decreases your objectivity, as with Peter or Malcolm's counsellor. Or it may be because a public direction shift may be subtle (as with Andrew, page 107) and its identification depends on evidence from an assessment of your own public–personal equilibrium in order to locate that of your clients. You may feel unconfident about using such 'subjective' evidence, especially if you lack experience of applying knowledge in this way. In Andrew's case, his counsellor was not aware of Andrew's shift towards public dominance until he found himself in the corresponding position, without his usual personal level interaction involvement.

Taking stock

Peter's quiet and apparently composed response to his client's angry outburst might be termed 'taking stock'. It represents a kind of masterly inactivity or psychological containment (see Bion, 1963). To an onlooker, its overt public level manifestation might appear to be unremarkable. In Peter's situation, however, he was both struggling to identify the nature of his personal reaction and trying to ensure that his associated emotions did not overspill into the public level, where they may have had an adverse effect on the transaction. In the short term, taking stock can provide time within the counselling transaction, to allow tempers to cool, for example. As with Peter and his client, a decrease in the highly charged emotional situation may allow for the return of a more rational approach and the restoration of ordinary therapeutic work. An avoidance of an automatic reaction on your part, which could be simply retaliatory, may be sufficient to return the transaction to within normal limits.

In the face of her clients' aggression, Barbara remained cut off from her personal reaction to her client until it adversely affected her public level functioning, manifested in her difficulty with remembering the content of her sessions. Supervision of her work helped Barbara to be in touch with the fear which she could not experience when seeing her client, and it showed to her the extent to which she had departed from her usual public level, resulting in her excessively questioning her client. She had not recognized that this style was different from her usual public level functioning and that it was this which was evoking an aggressive response from her client. When she understood the interaction more fully, her interrogatory style diminished and, although she felt more anxious during the sessions, she noticed that her client became less defensively aggressive. In this example, the restoration of the public–personal equilibrium to the straightforward did not involve Barbara discussing her view of the transaction's state of disequilibrium with her client. Rather, through supervision, Barbara was able to formulate the interaction problem more clearly to herself and this allowed her to alter her behaviour in the session with a beneficial effect on the straightforwardness of the counselling transaction.

Often there is either no such beneficial outcome or only a transient improvement in the transaction, in terms of its becoming un-complicated. Continually containing difficult thoughts or emotions without a ready outlet or way to understand their origins is emotionally draining. As your capacity to contain these feelings and states is limited, it is desirable to discuss problematic personal level situations before serious deterioration develops, departures become significant or emotions erupt dramatically into dangerous and damaging behaviour. Peter felt that he had only narrowly avoided a major confrontation with his client, which could have had a damaging outcome. Often, supervision is the place to discuss the timing and content of an intervention designed to raise the interpersonal issue on to the public level agenda of the transaction, where it might also become part of a negotiated therapeutic goal.

Where you have identified one of the three basic interaction patterns and judged that the transaction is not immediately threatened by a dangerous departure (*unlike* Peter's situation, see page 2), you may be able to use your insight to formulate the interaction pattern and to discuss this in relation to your clients' important interactions with key people in their past. Most often the relevant past interactions will be those involving parents or their substitutes. As these interactions tend to become recurring topics during the course of much counselling, you will be likely to have plenty of opportunities to make your interventions and do not need to be too hasty to intervene.

Actively intervening

Formulating the interaction pattern

Your interventions will be aimed at removing the adverse effect of the enacted basic interaction pattern, since, by this stage, it is as if the counselling relationship has become part of your clients' problem rather than its solution (Lockwood, 1992). To achieve this you either need to bring relevant personal level departures to the fore or, alternatively, to rid the transaction of inappropriate personal aspects which may be present in excess or may mask more appropriate issues. How you achieve this will vary and depends upon many factors, including the clarity and specificity of your formulations of the enacted basic interaction pattern. Where you have only a vague or incomplete formulation, however, you may still be able to convey the gist of the interpersonal difficulties to your clients. Indeed, it may sometimes be more useful for your formulation to be 'roughly right' than to be 'precisely wrong'.

> *At the second assessment interview, Peter was able to make a simple formulation, linking his view of the unsatisfactory first interview and his client's previous failed attempts to obtain professional help, as a result of the absence of an appropriate level of trust.*
>
> *Peter (15 minutes into the second interview): I heard you say just now that X had not helped you. Last week I remember you mentioned Y and Z as not being of any use. I thought that you did not seem to find me helpful or even trustworthy. I*

guess that it might be difficult for you, generally, trusting other people. I wonder what you think?

Conveying the essence of your formulation, as Peter did, may enable you to raise the potentially relevant issue without being too contentious. So, even if your clients do not agree with your formulation, it does not necessarily generate further interpersonal problems through causing offence. It is easier for your clients to accept or disregard your intervention if it is put simply and with a spirit of enquiry rather than of conviction about the truth of the matter. This is especially relevant when you see the need to intervene early on in a transaction in which you have little knowledge and experience of one another.

With clients whose personality development is more mature than that of Peter's client, you might choose a detailed intervention based on a more complex formulation, for example, linking the clients' current mistrust or misperception to its origins in a problematic relationship with an absent or neglectful parent.

In supervision, Helen's counsellor began to understand that, unwittingly, he had been led more by his emotions than by his professional judgement in agreeing to accompany Helen to the cemetery. He thus became aware of how responsible he had felt for making Helen feel 'better' and for helping to put matters right for her. His supervisor pointed out that he was almost accepting a parental role with respect to his client and that this might be because it was this which Helen craved, albeit ambivalently, particularly so since she had lost her actual relationship with her father. Counsellor and supervisor, following discussion, decided that in view of the blurring of the professional and personal boundaries within the counselling transaction, it might be helpful to link Helen's current need for, and attraction towards, her counsellor with the earlier loss of her father. The supervisor suggested that something along the following lines should be said to Helen.

Counsellor: You seem to be much more cheerful following the visit to the cemetery, but, I wonder if this is 'too good to be true' and that what has happened, in your mind, is that I have become a kind of father-substitute. If I were to become more of a father and less of a counsellor to you, however, I don't believe that I would be able to help you with your feelings surrounding the death of your father. Indeed, it might

> *become even harder to experience feelings of loss and there-*
> *fore take longer for you to come to terms with your father's*
> *death.*

Communicating your formulation involves attention to both timing
and style of delivery so that your clients are facilitated in listening
non-defensively. Many clients do not have a secure personality
development and find it hard to concentrate on what you say,
especially when feeling anxious, as they may be early on in the
counselling session or within the counsellor–client relationship.

Short interventions are easier to hear, such as a single phrase
'difficult trusting' in the context of Peter's transaction. A sentence
like 'It's almost as if I am expected to become your parent or even
your partner, not your counsellor', with Helen, may make the point
more effectively than a whole paragraph. The lack of the pronoun
'you' in the phrase 'difficult trusting' may help you form an
empathic contact with clients whose hyper-sensitivity to criticism
seriously hampers their ability to form a trusting relationship. It
makes the point, roughly but not precisely, that *you* can
understand that *they* may have had difficulties in the past which
continue into the present with you. In using such a short phrase,
therefore, you do not appear to be parading your counselling
prowess in a way which might evoke envy or admiration, which
can quickly turn into denigration. Many clients are prepared to 'cut
off their nose to spite their face' and it is important, therefore, that
you do not provide them, unwittingly, with opportunities to do so.
There may also be a place for humour, preferably not sarcasm, but
this should not be over-used. The hypothetical statement to Helen
might have been delivered with lightness, once her counsellor's
zeal had diminished.

Enhancing the personal level

How you try to restore the public–personal equilibrium, by facili-
tating an infusion of appropriate personal aspects, will depend on
whether it is both of you or just one who needs to be more in
touch with the personal level. Any active intervention to restore the
equilibrium implies that you have recognized a shift, and this fact
may mean that you are returning towards your normal equilibrium
(see Figure 7.4a). Even though recognition alone is insufficient to
restore the equilibrium of the whole transaction, it may allow you,
as with Andrew's counsellor, to consider which personal level

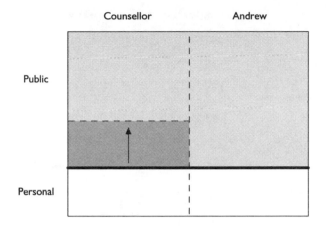

Figure 7.4a *Enhancing the personal level*

aspects might be missing and the relevance of their absence from the interaction, that is recognition helps you to begin to formulate the emotional content and meaning of the basic interaction pattern.

> *Andrew had told his counsellor that his parents had been 'local figures' in the small market town where he grew up. Their 'good works' took up much of their time, which might otherwise have been spent with Andrew and his younger sister. Consequently, both the children were frequently left to their own devices. It was at these times that Andrew first practised his delegation skills. He tended to order his sister about, but obtained little from this in terms of emotional comfort. He had only a vague recall of his childhood but remembered feeling lonely and always on the edge of social groups at school, never in the mainstream. His counsellor, in being unable to concentrate on Andrew, in effect became another emotionally absent parent.*

As a result of the above formulation, Andrew's counsellor felt more sympathetic towards Andrew. It allowed the former to understand more about the significance of an absence of personal level activity in the transaction. He kept this insight and formulation to himself, however, and gradually the transaction drifted back to the way it had been. Andrew remained cut off from his emotions and his

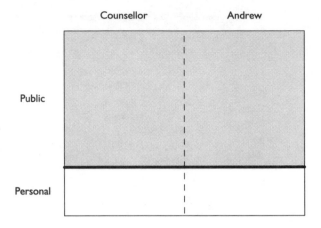

Figure 7.4b *Shift towards public dominance*

counsellor's empathic feelings ebbed away. His counsellor had slipped back into considering and planning his own life during their time together. Thus, both of them remained largely stuck with the equilibrium firmly shifted toward public dominance (see Figure 7.4b)

Malcolm was hardly in touch with his personal level, while his counsellor felt almost overwhelmed by her's (see Figure 7.5a). Eventually understanding and formulating the basic interaction pattern which was being enacted, allowed her to discuss the situation with Malcolm. This provided him with an opportunity to be more in touch with his personal feelings.

Twenty minutes into the session, Malcolm uncharacteristically fell silent. He had started as usual, somewhat passively, as if waiting for an invitation from his counsellor to detail his current worries. His counsellor obliged, as had become the pattern, by asking him how his last week had been and Malcolm was then launched into a familiar cycle of recounting his violent thoughts. His counsellor had noticed this repeating pattern and, on this occasion, formulated to herself what she thought the basic interaction pattern represented. Recognising the suitable pause, she then made the comment aloud that she often felt herself to be a helpless onlooker of

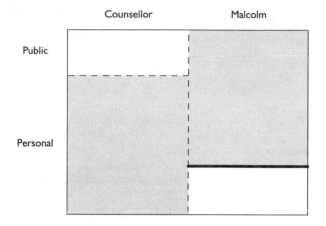

Figure 7.5a *Basic interaction pattern showing mixed dominance*

Malcolm's continuing difficulties and wondered if this was something he had felt as a child, confronted by his father's repeated violence towards his mother.

Counsellor: It sounds like you have had another bad week. Coming to these sessions seems not to help. It is as if I am not able to do anything to help you to improve matters, even though I can see how bad things are. I was wondering if this helplessness was like the helplessness you might have felt as a child, watching your parents fight.

Malcolm was taken aback by this empathic intervention and the feelings it evoked and, almost immediately, began to cry. Subsequently, his whole demeanour changed and he was able to move from simply listing his difficulties to talking about his past and the problematic relationships he had encountered growing up and more recently with his partner. He seemed to have spent most of his life feeling unable to influence people and events around him (see Figure 7.5b).

Thinking about the nature of the basic interaction pattern can be equally difficult, whether your shifted equilibrium has locked you into the public level or made you feel overwhelmed by feelings in the personal level, irrespective of whether the feelings involved are positive, as with Helen's counsellor, or negative, as with Peter.

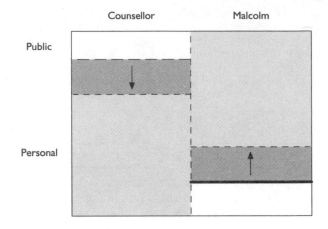

Figure 7.5b *Shifts towards a straightforward transaction*

Supervision of your work provides you with an opportunity to combine and integrate your intellectual and emotional capacities when you are, ideally, in a more relaxed state and part of a straightforward transaction with your supervisor!

It is important to note that with Malcolm's counsellor's intervention, when she talked of feeling like an onlooker, she did not reveal the full extent and nature of her own personal state. For Malcolm to know how impotent and hopeless his counsellor had felt would not necessarily have helped him to understand any more clearly the nature of his problem or his part in its maintenance. It might have served to blur the distinction in his mind between his counsellor as a person and as a professional. The result could have undermined the transaction (see Chapter 1). Such a revelation might only have made him feel victorious or guilty for causing his counsellor's discomfort. You therefore need to find a way of using your personal reaction, as Malcolm's counsellor did, to *inform* your intervention, so your clients have new opportunities to learn and are not left feeling inappropriately burdened or blamed. As with Peter, you may choose to wait for your usual emotional sensitivity and reactivity to return before intervening.

If there is little or no subsiding of the strength of your personal reaction during the session, or if the same pattern of reacting repeatedly occurs, then it is important to try to understand the origins of the departure from the straightforward counselling transaction through discussion during supervision. Various hypotheses may be entertained and it might be particularly useful to consider the possible effects of a variety of interventions through the construction of transaction windows, which can aid thinking about their likely interactive impact on the transaction (see Chapter 1, page 6).

Constraining the personal level

With supervision, Malcolm's counsellor was relatively soon able to recognize how imprisoned she felt in her personal level. Helen's counsellor, by contrast, was quite oblivious to his position for a considerable period. Whereas Malcolm's counsellor struggled with her feelings of inadequacy and impotence, Helen's counsellor behaved as if imbued with energy and enthusiasm to rescue his client against all the odds. Realizing how you have departed at the personal level, whether being paralysed or, alternatively, energized by unusual personal aspects, is important, so that the public–personal equilibrium can be restored by attempting to constrain the intensity of your clients' personal level contributions.

When, in her second interview, Barbara's client had revealed details of her sexual abuse, she had concluded that her initial pessimism about working with this client had been misplaced and was unjustified. Her client had sobbed as she recounted more and more detailed and explicit personal material. It was only when Barbara realized that she felt emotionally numbed by this superficially poignant account that she began to take stock of the overall situation within the transaction. (The client had been sexually abused by a group of men, only some of whom had actively assaulted her.) Listening to her client, Barbara noticed that, intermittently, she felt very attentive but at other times she felt strangely remote. She also felt pressurized to understand instantly how her client's current difficulties were linked to her previous abuse. Barbara realized, however, that she was not clear and that she could not be expected to understand fully. Sensing that all was not straightforward, Barbara decided to intervene.

Barbara: I think that what you are saying is very important. There is very much more that you may need to say about all of this and perhaps other areas of your past. At the moment, I'm not sure that we can really feel the full weight of what you are saying. Perhaps we need to recognize that we shall have many months to work together to try to fully understand what has gone on and how it is still affecting you today.

Initially, Barbara's client was not able to accept what her counsellor had said. She expressed her frustration and disappointment that she had been interrupted in mid-flow. Barbara, therefore, attempted to repeat her view but more concisely.

Barbara: I think you are trying too hard. Let's slow down. We'll need to use a lot of time to go over these important things.

Barbara's client now seemed more relaxed and, paradoxically, Barbara felt herself to have more time to think and to be in touch with feelings, particularly of sadness. Barbara wondered if, in talking about her past, albeit in an apparently animated and emotion-laden manner, her client had avoided contact with depressive feelings and thoughts, including pessimism about the counselling relationship itself. Her client's clear change, in response to Barbara's repeated intervention and the subsequent movement in the transaction towards the straightforward, allowed Barbara to regain some of her optimism that they might achieve something in working together.

Summary

Actively intervening in complicated counselling transactions, which have resisted a range of interventions designed to clarify, re-define or limit your respective roles and the goals you have agreed to pursue, is important but potentially problematic. Basic interaction patterns which underpin such departures are fuelled by powerful interpersonal influences stemming from longstanding aspects of your's and your clients' personalities. Sometimes these are also reinforced by current contextual influences serving the same ends.

Even though some basic interaction patterns may be relatively easy to identify, this does not make them easy to deal with. Indeed, some of the most obviously complicated transactions are the hardest to resolve. Essentially, having identified the basic inter-action pattern, you need to formulate its meaning through considering how it is affecting your thoughts, feelings and actions, and how this might relate to your clients. You may wish to tell your clients about your understanding of how the particular interaction pattern is adversely affecting the successful pursuit of mutually agreed transaction goals and, because it is rooted in past interactions, how it may also be playing a part in maintaining their presenting problems.

To accomplish all of this you need to be familiar with how a range of departures can be manifested in a public–personal disequilibrium. However, when this is so, your usual capacity for integrating your intellectual judgement with your emotional reaction, will often have been lost. Initially, therefore, you need to regain some of your usual public–personal equilibrium through considering the state of the transaction during and between sessions or during supervision. You are then in a position more accurately to evaluate your clients and their parts in the transaction and, only then, can you formulate the nature of the basic interaction pattern and decide how you might use this to inform your intervention. There will be transactions in which your best efforts to intervene to restore the public–personal equilibrium, and hence the overall straightforward character of the counselling transaction, are thwarted. You will have no option but to consider termination or transfer to another professional or agency (see later chapters).

8

Utilizing Contextual Influences

In this chapter we discuss how you can make use of the context in which the counselling transaction takes place. By context we refer to the social systems and interpersonal relationships in which both you and your clients are involved, aspects of which can influence the counselling transaction. In order to use these contextual influences you need to be aware that a change in your own context may influence those of your clients and vice versa, through an effect on the counselling transaction itself.

Before making therapeutic use of influences deriving from your clients' wider contexts, you need to evaluate your own contextual influences, such as those arising from the relationship with your immediate work colleagues, which could be exerting an adverse effect, making you depart from your usual professional style and emotional disposition. If you identify significant adverse influences, you need to understand their origins and try to ameliorate their influence. Only then should you evaluate your clients' systems environments as a prelude to using their contextual influences to therapeutic effect (see Figure 8.1).

The counsellor's contextual influences

Interpersonal and social contextual influences, which you judge to be impinging on your ability to work effectively with particular clients, may need to be resolved. There are various ways to achieve this aim, which rely on your involving others who form part of the context but who are outside your immediate counselling transaction.

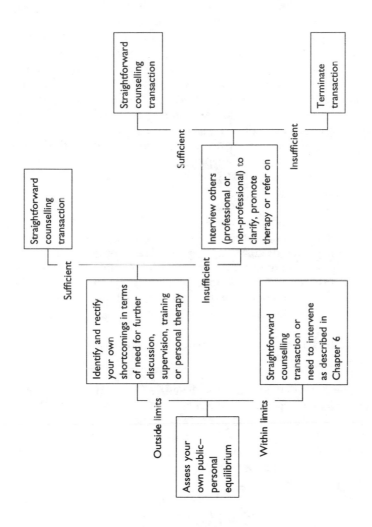

Figure 8.1 *Utilizing contextual influences*

Discussion

The contextual influences which impinge on you may be relatively discrete and easily resolved, such as a difference of opinion within your family or immediate professional colleagues which has left you angry or otherwise 'out of sorts' prior to counselling a client. The unhappy situation with Malcolm's counsellor and the family doctor (page 35) is an example where, even though the feelings involved were strong, it was a relatively simple matter for the counsellor and doctor to meet and to air their feelings and discuss differences, because their long-standing professional relationship was, ordinarily, a good one. As a result of their meeting, they readily regained their mutual respect and professional trust, also making arrangements to ensure that future referrals to the counsellor came with adequate supporting information concerning the clients' psychosocial contexts.

Supervision

Sometimes the complicating contextual influences cannot be so simply resolved by discussion. They may arise, for example, from a statutory requirement of your agreed terms of employment, which is not a matter of discussion or negotiation. Working in social services, probation, penal or forensic psychiatric settings, therefore, may mean that as part of your routine work you regularly encounter adverse influences, potentially complicating your counselling transaction, which originate from such immovable contextual factors. Peter, for example, was obliged by his probation work contract to see certain clients for 'therapy'. He had a well-established method for discussing issues concerning confidentiality, in which he stated the basis on which he might need to break the usual governing rules. Even though he was experienced in giving this explanation at the assessment interview, to orientate his client to the requirements of counselling, he was aware that he did not always cover all aspects with every client. With the particular client already referred to, Peter realized in retrospect that certain of his omissions in this area were serious and may well have contributed to (what he regarded as) the ultimately unfavourable outcome (see below).

When contextual influences, such as statutory obligations to counsel, cannot be avoided, their effects may still be ameliorated by consulting a senior colleague to discuss your therapeutic work and its associated difficulties or by obtaining more formal supervision of your work with particular clients.

Further training

Another option, especially when complicating contextual influences exist as part of your professional post, is to consider whether further professional training might be beneficial. There are many methods of training, differing in their psychological sophistication, theoretical orientation and intensity, in terms of the time commitment they demand. Some are short courses which focus on a particular topic, such as 'managing violence'. Others address a range of topics or clinical areas through theoretical seminars and supervised work with 'training cases', stretching over a period of years. (Such long-term work with particular clients can provide a good opportunity to witness the effect of your's or your clients' external life events on the counselling transaction, that is to observe and experience the effect of a range of contextual influences.) Some training courses require you to receive extensive personal psychotherapy as a requirement of acceptance, which continues until you qualify (see Wilkins, 1997). Further training may enhance the development of your skills beyond those of individual counselling, so enabling you to work with groups, couples and whole families.

Personal therapy

You may choose to have personal psychotherapy to understand or find a resolution to your individual responses to problematic or immovable contextual influences, as well as or instead of the above methods. This can be particularly relevant when you are already aware of your own significant personal conflicts, generated or maintained by the different systems to which you belong. Peter, for example, was attracted to his job as probation officer because of a desire to 'free people' from institutional incarceration. Sometimes his personal goal, which overlapped with that of his post, was achieved. Often, however, he found himself involved in decisions which returned his clients to the courts, either for sentencing to imprisonment or which resulted in their being moved to a higher, rather than lower, level of secure accommodation. This meant that Peter struggled with issues engendered by his professional situation which he found personally abhorrent. He was able to express some of his distress and to understand something of his wish to 'free people' during his personal therapy. He realized that this apparently noble but externally directed goal of freeing other people derived partly from his own personal difficulty with freely expressing his own negative emotions.

There is a wide range of personal therapies available which have different theoretical underpinnings and are conducted in different modalities, for example, group or family. Many are long-term and, if private, financially expensive. You would do well to research the options and their implications before embarking!

Referring on

You may wish to involve others in your wider professional systems to arrange a transfer or referral to them, if you recognize that your clients need a different approach. You will need to establish that the other person (or institution) is indeed appropriately placed to meet the needs of your clients, hence the initial contact is unlikely to include your clients. Once the appropriateness has been established, however, it may be important for all of you to meet together (that is including the client) to minimize the potential for misunderstanding or inadequate communication and to maximize appropriate expectations of the new professionals, therapy or institution. Explaining and ensuring that the rationale for the referral and transfer is understood by everyone may prevent further departures.

Transfers involve both endings and beginnings and may be painful and problematic. This is not necessarily so, however, and a meeting of all concerned can go some way to minimizing clients' distress and anxiety, even if they are left with some negative feelings.

> *After a scheduled break in therapy, Peter's client returned in a highly disturbed state. He appeared anxious and agitated, unable to remain seated for more than a few minutes at a time. His speech was fast, sometimes too fast for Peter to understand even the gist of what was being said. Peter's efforts to calm his client were unsuccessful and he wondered whether his client had taken illicit stimulant drugs, which might account for this overall presentation of such an altered appearance and behaviour. Initially, Peter's questions about drug-taking went unanswered. Then, his client became verbally abusive, stating that drugs were much more reliable*

and 'truer friends' than Peter was or ever could be. This was the only coherent statement Peter heard, after which his client left the room.

Peter wrote to his client stating his concern and his wish to re-evaluate the need for more intensive help, reminding him of their next appointment to meet. To Peter's surprise, his client attended. He seemed slightly less agitated but his speech was still fast and difficult to comprehend. He was able to confide, however, that he felt confused and frightened and he agreed to a meeting with a psychiatrist, which Peter arranged for later that week. The psychiatrist offered Peter's client in-patient treatment, which the latter accepted.

Over the next two months Peter met with his client in hospital, working solely to terminate their counselling trans-action. The period of his statutory responsibility towards his client had ended. It became clear that his client's mental health was likely to remain very poor, even after his with-drawal from all illicit drugs. The arrangement to terminate counselling did not seem to affect his client in any obvious way. Peter, however, felt depressed by what he himself con-sidered to be a professional failure.

The transaction with Barbara and her client also required the involvement of others, in this instance, the staff of a psychiatric day hospital. This followed an overdose of unprescribed medication and continuing suicidal ideation which hostel staff felt required more intensive psychiatric support. Barbara continued to see her client while she attended the day hospital, but less frequently than usual. After six months' attendance, Barbara's client was dis-charged and her counselling was resumed on its former basis.

The clients' contextual influences

You are most likely to consider utilizing your clients' contextual influences when the transaction has become complicated and when other interventions, such as the above or those discussed in Chapters 6 and 7, have failed to restore the straightforward trans-action. The main indication is, therefore, a failure of other inter-ventions. The involvement of others from the clients' wider interpersonal and social systems serves three main aims:

- Clarification
- Promoting therapy
- Ending.

Clarification

The first aim is to establish, by interviewing others with the consent of your clients, a better understanding of the origin and effect of complicating influences, especially those deriving from the transaction's wider interpersonal and social systems themselves. This is with the further aim of resolving them. (NB. The 'others' may include your clients' families, friends or other involved non-professionals.)

> *At the meeting she had called to complain to the family doctor that he had withheld useful information from her about their mutual client, Malcolm's counsellor suggested that the next step was to try to set up a meeting between themselves and Malcolm and his partner, so that a consistent and concerted approach could be agreed and implemented. Much to her surprise, Malcolm agreed to invite his partner, who accepted with only slight hesitation. Both Malcolm and his partner seemed to feel that they were being taken seriously by the professionals' call for this additional meeting.*
>
> *At the meeting, the doctor was able to state that Malcolm and his partner did have a valid benefits claim, without needing to exaggerate or falsify their actual situations. They were then able to see how mistrust had developed, leaving the doctor and, later, the counsellor feeling hoodwinked and Malcolm and his partner feeling misunderstood and patronized. The counsellor stated that she felt that the discussion freed herself and Malcolm to concentrate on his problematic nightmares and violent thoughts. Both Malcolm and his partner admitted, with embarrassment, that the counselling had already been of some benefit.*

Although many combinations of 'others' from the clients' wider social systems may be usefully involved, the total numbers in any meeting should be kept as low as possible. It is more important to have the most appropriate people present than settling for larger numbers of more peripherally involved people, as a substitute. Indeed, you may need to delay a meeting if this can guarantee that all the relevant personnel can be present.

Promoting therapy

In addition to increasing your understanding of complicating contextual influences by interviewing others, a second aim might be to persuade the others to act to safeguard or promote the counselling. There are two routes to achieving this outcome which you may pursue individually, sequentially or in tandem. The first is to use healthy contextual resources, whether from family or friends, separately or in combination, to bolster appropriate public level activity. The second is to limit complicating influences by encouraging others to alter particular attitudes or desist from certain behaviours or to make other changes. The first set of objectives relates to the support of the overall straightforward character of the counselling transaction, while the second to that of constraining complicating influences. Occasionally, other involved people are encouraged to function in the role of an 'auxiliary counsellor' in between the counselling sessions. The following examples show how others can be enlisted to support the transaction (Andrew) and how the effect of complicating influences can be resolved when limits are set and negative effects removed (Sheila).

> *Andrew's counsellor's initial optimism about his client's capacity to comprehend fully and participate in counselling turned to pessimism. Andrew seemed intent in turning the professional relationship into a personal one or, perhaps more accurately, one which was neither one nor the other. Such a hybrid of public and personal aspects seemed to be the trademark of most of Andrew's relationships. Andrew's wife alternated between playing the role of servant and wife. Likewise, Andrew's paid assistant had become his lover.*
>
> *Reflecting on the above issues and the questions they raised, the counsellor decided to deliver an ultimatum to Andrew. He stated that the counselling process between them was at a stalemate, which he believed could only be unlocked by his meeting Andrew's whole family – his wife and their two children. If Andrew did not agree to this plan, then there would be no other option than to terminate counselling. Andrew immediately protested at the unfairness of such a unilateral declaration. To the surprise of his counsellor, however, he suddenly stopped objecting and agreed to the meeting.*

The counsellor, who had only a limited experience of family therapy, lacked confidence about what he would say or do at the meeting. He felt his main insight was noticing how Andrew conflated his professional and personal relationships. At the meeting the counsellor decided to make three introductory statements. First, he said that Andrew's therapy was not working. Secondly, he stated that he felt everybody in the family was affected by or involved in Andrew's problems in some way. Thirdly, he stated that Andrew seemed to have no clear boundary between professional and personal aspects in his relationships. His counsellor ended by saying that Andrew was 'at work while he was at home and more at home when he was at work'. Having said all of this, the counsellor himself wondered exactly what he had meant by the last phrase and feared that it would mystify or bemuse Andrew and his family.

Andrew slowly covered his face with his hands and began to sob uncontrollably. This situation continued for a few minutes with nobody in the room moving. Finally, it was Andrew's son who got up from his chair and put a hand on his father's shoulder. The daughter was now weeping silently. The wife, who had turned away from her husband, stared stonily out of the window.

In the latter part of the meeting, it became clear that the counsellor's insight was accurate but painful for Andrew to hear and for his children and later also his wife to endorse. It was agreed that husband and wife had much to talk about and that they should meet with the counsellor and a female colleague for some exploratory marital sessions. The aim of these sessions would be to see if there were sufficient warmth and mutual respect to resurrect Andrew's marriage.

Obviously, involving family members in order to support the counselling transaction does not always have such a dramatic impact. In this instance, however, the intervention seemed to unlock a complicated counselling transaction which had become stuck. In the case of Sheila, the aim was different, namely, to involve family members to constrain complicating influences.

Sheila's counsellor felt that counselling was not progressing adequately in spite of a helpful discussion about the power relationships within the family. She believed that Sheila's inability or refusal to confide personal material, for example, about her pregnancy and its termination, meant that the counselling itself might need to be aborted. The counsellor was reluctant to suggest this, however, since she vividly remembered how difficult it had been for Sheila to even enter the consulting room at their first meeting. She was determined not to give up without trying to understand more about why Sheila found it so hard to ask people for help and why she felt so guilty if she made critical comments about her mother or brother. The counsellor, having noted that talking about her relationship difficulties brought Sheila little relief, believed that she might be subject to pressures, adverse to the counselling transaction, resulting from the 'power' struggles within the family.

It took several sessions of her counsellor's coaxing to set up a meeting with Sheila, her mother and brother. On the day, all three were sullen and silent, leaving the therapist wondering why she had pressed so hard for this meeting. Sheila's brother was the first to speak, saying he was at his 'wit's end' and feeling bitterly disappointed with what he saw as the failure of counselling. He talked at length about professional and financial sacrifices he had made for the family. He had no answer, however, to the counsellor's enquiry about why he continued to put others' needs and wishes before his own, when he so clearly resented it.

In the rest of the session, it became clear that all the family members allowed themselves to be governed by guilt and how most of their communications were designed to evoke guilt in each other. Although they all agreed that they were miserable and did not really deserve to be so, nobody knew why they felt so guilty. When the topic of father's death emerged towards the end of the meeting they all broke down in tears. The origin of their guilty feelings appeared, at least in part, to be connected with this loss.

The family asked if they could have a second meeting. At this, the emotional atmosphere was lighter. They discussed how shocked they had been that they could openly grieve, express sadness and, notably, survive the experience relatively intact. In fact, they each felt more self-confident. Mother gave 'permission' for her son to leave home, although she seemed to believe that Sheila would always remain with her. As her individual therapy continued, thereafter, Sheila was freer to

> *speak about her family and other personal matters, without*
> *her usual reserve and guilt.*

The grip of the complicating contextual influences on the counselling transaction were consequently lessened through involving
Sheila's mother and brother. With other clients, it might be
appropriate to use a combination of the two above approaches
involving others, the one aiming to support directly the public level
of the transaction (as with Andrew) and the other aimed at minimizing or removing the effects of complicating contextual
influences (as with Sheila). The effect of one approach may lead
to the recognition of the additional need for the other.

Ending

The third aim is to involve others in a discussion about ending the
transaction. Endings may be planned and occur when you have
achieved your counselling goals or they may arise, often with little
warning, when counselling is breaking down. In the latter situation
it may still be possible to set and work towards an agreed ending
date, even if this is only a few sessions away.

The ending of Malcolm's counselling was planned. After the
meeting with Malcolm, his partner and the family doctor, considerable headway was made with his nightmares and daytime
violent thoughts and aggressive outbursts. The reasons for this
improvement, however, were not entirely clear. Malcolm's partner
had successfully given birth to a baby girl and all concerned were
in good health. Their relationship, as a couple, had improved. With
Malcolm's consent, the views of the social workers who were
overseeing the parenting of Malcolm's daughter were sought. They
reported the development of a healthy relationship between both
parents and between parents and their baby. They themselves
claimed to have a good relationship with Malcolm and his partner.
On the basis of this positive report and the sustained improve-
ments in the clients' nightmares and violent thoughts, the counsellor concluded that no further progress was likely and that she
and Malcolm should work to an agreed end-date. Malcolm
appeared to be genuinely grateful for the help that he had received
and, at the last session, he presented his counsellor with a card in
which he and his partner thanked her for her patience and help.

Summary

The counselling transaction is subject to myriad contextual influences which interact to support or undermine the straightforward pursuit of transaction goals. By involving relevant people from either your own context or those of your clients, you may be able to alter the balance of the competing influences so as to minimize complicating factors or promote the straightforward counselling transaction. You may wish to involve other people early in the counselling transaction, even in the assessment phase. Alternatively, and more commonly, they become involved only after interventions have failed. Your interventions involving others derive from how you formulate the origins, function and type of complicating factor.

The utilization of your own context involving wider professional systems to resolve complicating influences differs from how you use and involve your clients' wider systems. With the former, you involve others to clarify complicating aspects, to provide supervision, further professional training or personal therapy, or to refer on to them. With the latter, you involve others to clarify the nature and extent of a complicating aspect, to deal with this aspect in order to promote the beneficial effects of counselling or to help you make a decision regarding the termination of the counselling.

9

Interface with Other Models

In the course of your work, you may encounter different models of working with clients, as well as a variety of other professionals who inevitably use a wide range of technical language. In this chapter we consider how concepts from other models can relate to or be construed in terms of the counselling transaction model. The concepts chosen are those which are commonly associated with clients who are perceived to be 'difficult'.

If you work in conjunction with healthcare professionals, you may encounter the psychiatric diagnostic term 'personality disorder' to refer to such clients. If your work also brings you into contact with the criminal justice system or you work exclusively within that system, you will need to understand the legal category of 'psychopathic disorder', which may apply to some of your clients. If you regularly refer to, or get referrals from, clinical psychologists, psychodynamic psychotherapists or psychoanalysts, you will probably meet the term 'borderline personality', whose meaning is often unclear.

Such terms do not correspond exactly with those of the counselling transaction model since they are exclusively client-focused. Thus, personality disorder, psychopathic disorder and borderline personality, as they do not have equivalents within any relational model, require extrapolation if they are to complement the model. This is particularly so since these same terms are also often mis-applied, sometimes pejoratively.

In order to communicate effectively about mutual clients when working with other professionals, you will need to know how far you have a shared understanding of concepts and terms. You will also need to be able to reconcile disparate aspects of the different models whenever possible, and to recognize when it is impossible to do so.

This final chapter is organized according to the three systems referred to: the healthcare system; the criminal justice system; and the wider psychotherapy system. The highlighted terms are defined to prevent misunderstanding and are discussed to explore the extent to which their application can complement the use of the counselling transaction model.

The healthcare system

Some of your clients, who are or who have been in the healthcare system, may well have had their personal and social deficits diagnosed in terms of personality disorder (American Psychiatric Association, 1994; WHO, 1992).

Personality disorder

In the *International Classification of Diseases* (ICD-10) (WHO, 1992), a diagnosis of personality disorder is defined as:

> deeply ingrained and enduring behaviour patterns, manifesting themselves as inflexible responses to a broad range of personal and social situations. They represent either extreme or significant deviations from the way the average individual in a given culture perceives, thinks, feels and particularly relates to others. Such behaviour patterns tend to be stable and to encompass multiple domains of behaviour and psychological functioning. They are frequently, but not always, associated with various degrees of subjective distress and problems in social functioning and performance. (WHO, 1992: 200)

In the *Diagnostic and Statistical Manual of Mental Disorders* (DSM-IV) (American Psychiatric Association, 1994) personality disorder is defined as:

A. An enduring pattern of inner experience and behavior that deviates markedly from the expectations of the individual's culture. This pattern is manifested in two (or more) of the following areas:
   (1) cognition (i.e., ways of perceiving and interpreting self, other people, and events)
   (2) affectivity (i.e., the range, intensity, lability and appropriateness of emotional response)
   (3) interpersonal functioning
   (4) impulse control.

B. The enduring pattern is inflexible and pervasive across a broad range of personal and social situations.

C. The enduring pattern leads to clinically significant distress or impairment in social, occupational, or other important areas of functioning.

D. The pattern is stable and of long duration and its onset can be traced back at least to adolescence or early adulthood.

E. The enduring pattern is not better accounted for as a manifestation or consequence of another mental disorder.

F. The enduring pattern is not due to the direct physiological effects of a substance (e.g., a drug of abuse, a medication) or a general medical condition (e.g., head trauma). (American Psychiatric Association, 1994: 633)

Each definition implies or refers directly to interpersonal difficulties, as one of the core defining characteristics of personality disorder. Such difficulties vary in extent and are differently expressed according to the sub-category of personality disorder (see Table 9.1).

The diagnostic label of personality disorder can be of value to clinicians, if it is accurately applied, as a convenient descriptive shorthand to aid communication. However, its misapplication, because of an inadequate diagnostic assessment or from a sense of therapeutic frustration, may stigmatize clients. The label personality disorder can imply that clients are untreatable or undeserving of the usual treatment or services which are afforded to other clients (Lewis and Appleby, 1988).

To make a diagnosis of personality disorder, the clinician has to consider many aspects of the patients' past and current personal and social functioning, tracing evidence of any deficit found continuously back in the individuals' histories. This is to establish that it is indeed related to enduring personality characteristics and not simply a reaction to exceptional or episodic situations or stresses, such as the effects of illness or addiction. The diagnostic process often requires the clinician to interview the individuals on more than one occasion and to collect information from other informants, such as family members (Norton, 1996). If clients are referred to you with a 'diagnosis' of personality disorder, yet without evidence of an adequate diagnostic process having been followed, you may need to consider whether the label of personality disorder has been inappropriately assigned.

The sub-categories of personality disorder, even within a single system of classification (ICD-10 or DSM-IV), are not mutually

Table 9.1 *Comparison of current classification of personality disorder sub-types (adapted from Tyrer, 1991)*

	ICD-10		DSM-IV
Code	Description	Code	Description
F60.0	*Paranoid* – excessive sensitivity, suspiciousness, preoccupation with conspiratorial explanation.	301.00	*Paranoid* – interpretation of people's actions as deliberately demeaning or threatening.
F60.1	*Schizoid* – emotional coldness, detachment, lack of interest in other people, eccentricity and introspective fantasy.	301.20	*Schizoid* – indifference to relationships and restricted range of emotional experience and expression.
–	No equivalent.	302.22	*Schizotypal* – deficit in inter-personal relatedness with peculiarities of ideation, appearance and behaviour.
F60.5	*Anankastic* – indecisiveness, doubt, excessive caution, pedantry, rigidity and need to plan in immaculate detail.	301.40	*Obsessive-compulsive* – pervasive perfectionism and inflexibility.
F60.4	*Histrionic* – self-dramatization, shallow mood, egocentricity and craving for excitement with persistent manipulative behaviour.	301.50	*Histrionic* – excessive emotionality and attention seeking.
F60.7	*Dependent* – failure to take responsibility for actions, with subordination of personal needs to those of others, excessive dependence with need for constant reassurance and feelings of helplessness when a close relationship ends.	301.60	*Dependent* – persistent dependent and submissive behaviour.
F60.2	*Dyssocial* – callous unconcern for others, with irresponsibility, irritability and aggression, and incapacity to maintain enduring relationships.	301.70	*Antisocial* – evidence of repeated conduct disorder before the age of 15 years.
–	No equivalent	301.81	*Narcissistic* – pervasive grandiosity, lack of empathy and hypersensitivity to the evaluation of others.

continued overleaf

Table 9.1   *(cont.)*

| ICD-10 | | DSM-IV | |
Code	Description	Code	Description
F60.6	*Anxious* – persistent tension, self-consciousness, exaggeration of risks and dangers, hypersensitivity to rejection, and restricted lifestyle because of insecurity.	301.82	*Avoidant* – pervasive social discomfort, fear of negative evaluation and timidity.
F60.30	*Impulsive* – inability to control anger, to plan ahead, or to think before acts, with unpredictable mood and quarrelsome behaviour.	301.83	*Borderline* – pervasive instability of mood and self-image.
F30.31	*Borderline* – unclear self-image, involvement in intense and unstable relationships.		

exclusive and some characteristics are common to more than one sub-category. This limits the usefulness of the terms. An alternative to the unreliability of sub-categorization is to view personality disorder as a single disorder (Coid, 1989). Accordingly, clients can be considered simply to have a diagnosis of personality disorder, if fitting the basic definition, whether or not the criteria required of any personality disorder sub-categories are achieved.

Although a carefully evaluated diagnosis of personality disorder may convey important information about how your clients are likely to appear and behave in certain circumstances, it cannot accurately predict your likely interaction with the clients in the counselling transaction. In this way, it differs from the 'diagnosis' of the complicated counselling transaction which both takes account of and applies to counsellor and clients, rather than solely to the clients. However, the two models, medical diagnosis and counselling transaction, can be applied together with benefit. This became clear, albeit with hindsight, in the case of Helen.

> *Helen's counsellor, who had become the object of his client's erotic interest, re-read her referrer's letter. In it, Helen had been described by her family doctor as displaying 'many features of a dependent personality disorder'. Her counsellor*

> *realized that he had missed the significance of this infor-*
> *mation. In constantly reassuring Helen, he had supported*
> *and bolstered only the less adaptive aspects of her personality.*
> *Trying to relieve her immediate distress, he had not helped her*
> *at all with her underlying personality difficulty. The issue of*
> *dependency, initially reflected in her failure to present her*
> *complaint adequately and to own responsibility for it, was not*
> *addressed as a potential, negotiated transaction goal.*

Helen's counsellor could have attached importance to the referrer's mention of personality disorder and, assuming there was no reason to doubt its validity, this diagnostic term would have provided him with information which could have guided his approach to Helen. It would have alerted him to the particular way in which the transaction between the two of them might have been likely to depart from the straightforward, even though it would not have alerted him specifically to the eroticization of their relationship. Even if he had failed to notice any of its signs at the beginning, such as his own failure to expect her to be able to provide adequate personal information, Helen's counsellor might have recognized the departures sooner and introduced to the public level agenda the issue of his clients' passivity and maladaptive dependence as potential transaction goals.

Although few of your clients are likely to fit perfectly the criteria for a single sub-category of personality disorder, being aware of your clients' personality disorder characteristics and knowing your likely reaction to the expression of such aspects could help you to avoid or identify departures from the straightforward transaction. This would pave the way for such interpersonal aspects to become negotiated transaction goals or be dealt with via the setting of appropriate limits or the use of a therapy contract (see Chapter 6).

The criminal justice system

Some clients with disordered personalities may express their problems in anti-social, violent or other criminal ways which attract the attention of the criminal justice system. Merely criminalizing their behaviour and labelling it solely as 'bad', however, does not help you face the therapeutic challenge posed by such clients. Part of the therapeutic task is to understand the psychological motivation for and personal meaning of your clients' overt behaviour, the aim being that such understanding will provide the clients with more choice and self-control so that in the future they will have less need to resort to such behaviours. To effect this requires the clients to have some desire to understand the origins of their behaviour and sufficient psychological resources to inhibit impulses to act violently or criminally, as well as some capacity to verbalize painful emotional conflicts.

Psychopathic disorder
The criminal justice system's primary concern is with behavioural facts and moral judgements, not with an understanding of psychological motivation or personal meaning. This focus is reflected in the legal definition of 'psychopathic disorder', which is defined as:

> a persistent disorder or disability of mind (whether or not including a significant impairment of intelligence) which results in abnormally aggressive or seriously irresponsible conduct on the part of the person concerned. (Mental Health Act, 1983: Part I, p. 2)

In other words, the legal definition of psychopathic disorder, which may apply to a client of yours, predominantly emphasizes observable behaviour of a specified kind. As a category it differs from a number of the sub-categories of personality disorder which have no requirement for such specific conduct to be present but which do specify certain psychological features to be present in order to qualify for the diagnosis (see Table 9.1, page 137).

If you are working with clients who have had or are in current contact with the criminal justice system, you will encounter the legal term psychopathic disorder. It is important that you are able to discern when the term is being used correctly, in its legal context, or is being misapplied. 'Psychopath', a noun derived from the legal term, is used stigmatically, not only by some members of the legal system but also by healthcare workers and others. Used in this way, it conveys 'badness' – dangerousness, unpredictability, untreatability or profound general unworthiness. As such, it does not reliably convey discrete information and cannot therefore aid professional communication or clinical management.

If your counselling work brings you into regular contact with the criminal justice system, as inevitably happens with those working in the probation service or forensic psychiatry, you may feel the tension which comes from the potentially conflicting demands of the two (hierarchic and overlapping) systems. The criminal justice system expects you to protect society, shielding potential victims from your clients and invites you, at least to an extent, to stigmatize your clients by viewing them as deviant or 'bad'. The counselling or healthcare system, however, requires you to afford your clients the confidentiality and respect to which all clients are entitled, that is not to marginalize them or reflect prejudice and to be realistically optimistic about the potential success of the counselling transaction.

The differing goals of the two systems, which are often not made explicit, can complement one another, particularly when your clients are motivated to explore the origins of their anti-social behaviour and to change. Often, however, such harmonization of goals only develops after you have felt torn by your dual allegiances or your clients have begun to make progress as a result of counselling, which may have been extremely arduous. Sometimes no such concordance occurs. Feeling caught in the middle of the conflicting goals of the two (overlapping and, sometimes, hierarchically related) systems, you may feel as if you are failing everybody (see Chapter 3). At such times you may be under considerable pressure to view your clients in an 'either–or' way, that is they are evil perpetrators or innocent victims. It is important that you resist the temptation to simply construe them as one or the other (Norton and Dolan, 1995).

> *Peter felt a strong impulse to contact the police regarding his client, having heard of the attack on the offender which so closely mirrored that of his client on his foster father. Feeling personally affected, literally losing some sleep (see page 67), he discussed the matter in supervision with a senior probation colleague, and together they considered the advantages and disadvantages of such an action. They concluded that the client's past violence was only ever in the context of a sexually abusive relationship with his foster father and that the client would have been highly unlikely to have attacked a stranger (the offender referred to above), even one who shared some features with a previous victim. They thus decided not to inform the police.*

In not informing the police, Peter afforded his client the usual degree of confidentiality, but only after assessing meticulously his client's likely potential for violence in the light of details of his past and the current status of the counselling transaction with himself.

He remained aware of the dual responsibilities to client and society, which were imposed on him by his job as probation officer. Peter considered it important to inform his clients exactly when he would need to break confidentiality as part of their first interview. The issues surrounding confidentiality can thus become part of their negotiated public level agenda.

Situations like this, which involve a serious consideration of whether to breach the usual confidentiality, are relevant to work with all clients, not just those who have previously offended. Thus all counsellors need to be alert to the relevant issues.

The wider psychodynamic psychotherapy system

You may well come into contact with clinical psychologists or psychodynamic psychotherapists who use impenetrable psychodynamic jargon. It may be evident in the language they use in making their referral to you. Alternatively, if you turn to such a psychotherapist for supervision, you may find that they speak a different professional language from yourself. Often the psychotherapist will be willing and able to provide an adequate translation of any unfamiliar terminology and effective communication can be achieved. Sometimes the psychodynamic psychotherapy literature, to which you may turn for understanding, is unclear, so it may be helpful to consider how the counselling transaction and its associated concepts can be linked to some core psychodynamic concepts and terms relevant to so-called 'difficult clients'.

Borderline personality organization

Borderline personality organization (BPO) refers to a specific patterning within the mind resulting in an unstable, partial and extreme experience of, and relationship to, both the self and others and is frequently maladaptive. According to much psychoanalytic theory, BPO results from the over-deployment of immature psychological defence mechanisms erected early in life in the face of perceived or imagined psychological insult or privation (see Kernberg, 1975). Its behavioural expression varies but is often problematic, causing or maintaining interpersonal problems and a range of associated difficulties with intimate personal and wider social role relationships. This is because its manifestation is via ambivalence and extreme attitudes or is an oscillation between the two, all of which can adversely affect the quality of personal interaction (Norton, 1997). Not all individuals showing features of BPO, however, are personality disordered (see below).

As a measure of your clients' current psychological functioning, borderline personality organization (Kernberg, 1975) is more sensitive to change than a diagnosis of personality disorder, and hence is of greater potential use in counselling practice. Its particular relevance here is that clients functioning at this psychological level may well present 'of' themselves (see Chapter 4). They are thus less likely than those who can achieve neurotic personality organization (who can present 'from within') to perform the role of client straightforwardly and are more likely to participate in an enactment of one or more of the basic interaction patterns. Recognizing BPO phenomena in your clients may make your prediction of later significant departures in the counselling transaction more reliable.

Barbara did not appreciate the full extent of her client's borderline personality organization until the latter had started to attend the day hospital (page 127). At the first of the scheduled review meetings between Barbara and day hospital staff she discovered that her client had already revealed to the staff extensive details of her sexual abuse and had been in so much obvious emotional distress that in-patient admission had been considered. This information came as a surprise to Barbara since her client had become calmer and more articulate during their weekly sessions together which had continued.

At the review, the day hospital staff were sceptical of the value of Barbara's individual counselling sessions, noting how their mutual client tended to be 'even worse' on the day of an individual session. The staff implied that their own, more extended contact with the client, afforded by day hospital attendance, meant that they were in a better position than Barbara to judge their clients' actual psychological state and therapeutic needs. Barbara found herself feeling increasingly annoyed at the implicit devaluation of her own therapeutic efforts and at the staff's partial account, which was at odds with her own view, based on the recent sessions. She felt tempted to contradict the staff, claiming for herself a more prolonged and in-depth emotional contact with and understanding of their client! However, she continued to listen to the staff's account of the clients' progress or lack of it.

Barbara then recalled how she had interrupted her client's outpouring of emotion and detail regarding the sexual abuse, during the assessment period (page 119). She wondered whether her client might have used the day hospital environ- ment, especially the greater availability of staff time, in order to ventilate her pent-up feelings from the past. Having listened to the staff, Barbara gave them feedback about her recent sessions, in which her client had been relatively composed, but also indicated how the counselling had started with early access to 'deep' emotional material which was echoed in the client's entry to the day hospital. The staff realized that Barbara's initial experience was similar to their own in certain respects and that she offered a valuable complemen- tary perspective. They ceased to hold the view that they were the sole experts on their shared client. Between them they agreed that each had a role and that further review meetings would be required in order to continue to understand more of the whole complex picture of what was happening with their mutual client.

It is not unusual for certain staff working with the same clients to feel that they have special access to the client's personal infor- mation or to a deep emotional contact with the clients that the others do not (Main, 1957). This situation is more likely to occur with those clients who function at a borderline personality organ- ization level, since their partial and extreme views of themselves are readily reciprocated, by at least some professionals who mistake such a partial representation for the whole. One result is that professionals conflict in their views over shared clients, as with Barbara and the day hospital staff, tending to view the same clients in opposing and extreme ways or taking the side of the clients against other professionals (Norton and Dolan, 1995). If such contradictory and partial views are not uncovered and resolved, the clients may receive an inconsistent delivery of whatever treatment approach is being applied. In this way, departures from the straightforward transaction are created or reinforced.

The recognition of relevant interpersonal evidence of borderline personality organization can therefore complement an application of the counselling transaction model by alerting you to the likelihood of significant departures. Barbara was able to recognize in the partial accounts from the day hospital staff, which differed so markedly from her own perception, how the client was functioning at a borderline personality organization level. During her initial silence, she was able to consider these issues and to avoid simply becoming embattled with the staff, which would have potentially undermined their much needed collaborative approach. Barbara's appreciation of the interpersonal enactment of her clients' borderline personality organization, which she eventually communicated to the day hospital staff, contributed to a fuller understanding of their mutual client.

Borderline phenomena may be suggested by a large number of aspects evident at interview, including at assessment, but only if you are aware of this possibility and able to elicit such evidence accurately. Some relevant aspects have been described earlier in this book, although not referred to as such (see especially Chapter 4, pages 48 to 57). Recognizing these will alert you to the increased possibility that significant departures from the straightforward counselling transaction could arise.

To elicit BPO phenomena reliably, you need to be aware of how certain psychoanalytic concepts, especially the unconscious psychological defence mechanisms of 'repression' and 'splitting', are manifested interpersonally at interview. You also require an ability to distinguish an integrated from a diffuse identity in your clients and be able to evaluate whether their reality testing is intact. How to do this is described in detail elsewhere (Kernberg, 1981).

BPO should be distinguished from borderline personality disorder (American Psychiatric Association, 1994), with which it is frequently confused. The latter is a psychiatric diagnostic term which refers to one particular sub-category of personality disorder (see Table 9.1, page 137). The diagnosis is made according to conventional medical diagnostic practice and does not rely on more specialized psychoanalytic language or skills, which are required to identify clients' levels of personality organization. If a colleague simply uses the adjective 'borderline', therefore, it is important to clarify to which term it applies, a sub-category of personality disorder or a level of personality organization.

Summary

In this chapter, we have highlighted some important areas of confusion in the definition and use of terminology applied to so-called 'difficult clients'. We have also shown how some of these client-focused terms can be used in conjunction with the counselling transaction model. Some of the terms may be new to the reader and, if so, the references mentioned can form an introduction to a more detailed reading on particular aspects.

The concepts associated with our counselling transaction model do not explain the total complexity of interpersonal processes which arise, even in straightforward counselling transactions. They do, however, recognize the inter-relatedness of public and personal level factors and the important interaction between the personalities of both counsellor and client. It is hoped that, irrespective of your prior training and theoretical orientation, when confronted with a 'difficult client', you will be able to apply the counselling transaction model with benefit.

References

Ainsworth, M.D.S. (1991) Attachments and other affectional bonds across the life cycle. In: *Attachment Across the Life Cycle*. Eds Parkes, C.M., Stevenson-Hinde, J. and Morris, P. London: Routledge. pp. 32–52.

American Psychiatric Association (1994) *Diagnostic and Statistical Manual of Mental Disorders* (4th edn) Washington, DC: American Psychiatric Association.

Asen, K., George, E., Piper, R. and Stevens, A. (1989) A systems approach to child abuse: management and treatment issues. *Child Abuse and Neglect*, 13: 45–58.

Bentovim, A. (1992) *Trauma-organised Systems: Physical and Sexual Abuse in Families*. London: Karnac Books.

Bentovim, A. (1996) Family therapy. In: *An Introduction to the Psychotherapies*. Ed. Bloch, S. Oxford: Oxford University Press. pp. 238–60.

Bion, W.R. (1963) *Elements of Psycho-analysis*. London: William Heinemann Medical Books Ltd.

Bloch, S. and Aveline, M. (1996) Group psychotherapy. In: *An Introduction to the Psychotherapies*. Ed. Bloch, S. Oxford: Oxford University Press. pp. 84–115.

Brooke, R. (1994) Assessment for psychotherapy: clinical indicators of self cohesion and self pathology. *British Journal of Psychotherapy*, 10 (3): 317–30.

Bowlby, J. (1969) *Attachment and Loss* (Vol. 1) Attachment. London: The Hogarth Press and the Institute of Psycho-analysis.

Bowlby, J. (1973) *Attachment and Loss* (Vol. 2) Separation: Anxiety and Anger. London: The Hogarth Press.

Carpy, D.V. (1989) Tolerating the countertransference: a mutative process. *International Journal of Psychoanalysis*, 70(2): 287–94.

Coid, J.W. (1989) Psychopathic disorders. *Current Opinion in Psychiatry*, 2: 750–6.

Coid, J.W. (1996) Dangerous patients with mental illnesses: increased risks warrant new policies, adequate resources and appropriate legal action. *British Medical Journal*, 312: 965–6.

Grounds, A. (1995) Risk assessment and management in clinical context. In: *Psychiatric Patient Violence – Risk and Response*. Crichton, S.J. London: Duckworth. pp. 43–59.

Hobbs, M. (1996) Short-term dynamic psychotherapy. In: *An Introduction to the Psychotherapies*. Ed. Bloch, S. Oxford: Oxford University Press. pp. 52–83.

Kernberg, O.F. (1975) *Borderline Condition and Pathological Narcissism*. New York: Jason Aronson Inc.

Kernberg, O.F. (1981) Structural interviewing. *Psychiatric Clinics of North America*, 1: 169–95.

Kernberg, O.F. (1989) The narcissistic personality disorder and the differential diagnosis of antisocial behavior. *Psychiatric Clinics of North America*, 12(3): 553–70.

Khan, M.M.R. (1983) On lying fallow. In: *Hidden Selves: Between Therapy and Practice in Psychoanalysis*. London: The Hogarth Press and the Institute of Psycho-analysis. pp. 183–88.

Lask, B. (1987) Family therapy. *British Medical Journal*, 294: 203–4.

Lewis, G. and Appleby, L. (1988) Personality disorder: the patients psychiatrists dislike. *British Journal of Psychiatry*, 153: 44–9.

Lockwood, G. (1992) Psychoanalysis and the cognitive therapy of personality disorders. *Journal of Cognitive Psychotherapy*, 6 (1): 25–47.

Main, T. (1957) The ailment. *British Journal of Medical Psychology*, 30: 129–45.

Mattinson, J. (1992) *The Reflection Process in Casework Supervision*. London: Institute of Marital Status.

Meissner, S.J., W.W. (1993) Treatment of patients in the borderline spectrum: an overview. *American Journal of Psychotherapy*, 47(2): 184–93.

Meloy, J.R. (1988) *The Psychopathic Mind: Origins, Dynamics and Treatment*. New York: Jason Aronson Inc.

Miller, L.J. (1989) In-patient management of borderline personality disorder: review and update. *Journal of Personality Disorders*, 3: 122–34.

Norton, K.R.W. (1996) Management of difficult personality disorder patients. *Advances in Psychiatric Treatment*, 2: 202–10.

Norton, K.R.W. (1997) In the prison of severe personality disorder. *Journal of Forensic Psychiatry*, 8:285–98.

Norton, K.R.W. and Dolan, B.M. (1995) Acting out and the institutional response. *Journal of Forensic Psychiatry*, 6: 317–32.

Norton, K.R.W. and Smith, S.P. (1994) *Problems with Patients: Managing Complicated Transactions*. Cambridge: Cambridge University Press.

Palmer, S. and MacMahon, G. (eds) (1997) *Client Assessments*. London: Sage.

Parsons, T. (1951) *The Social System*. New York: Free Press.

Prins, H. (1996) Risk assessment and management in criminal justice and psychiatry. *The Journal of Forensic Psychiatry*, 7(1): 42–62.

Royal College of Psychiatrists Special Working Party on Clinical Assessment and Management of Risk (1996) Council Report CR53, *Assessment and Clinical Management of Risk of Harm to Other People*. London: Royal College of Psychiatrists.

Searles, H.F. (1979) *Countertransference and Related Subjects*. New York: International University Press.

Sifnoes, P.E. (1973) The prevalence of alexithymia characteristics in psychosomatic patients. *Psychotherapy and Psychosomatics*, 22: 255–62.

Sills, C. (Ed.) (1997) *Contracts in Counselling*. London: Sage.

Sinason, V. (1992) *Mental Handicap and the Human Condition: New Approaches from the Tavistock*. London: Free Associations.

Temple, N. (1996) Transference and Countertransference: general and forensic aspects. In: *Forensic Psychotherapy: Crime, Psychodyamics and the Offender*

Patient (Vol. 1) *Mainly Theory*. Eds Cordess, C. and Cox, M. London: Jessica Kingsley Publishers. pp. 23–39.

Truax, C.B., Wargo, D.G., Frank, J.D., Imber, S.D., Battle, C.C., Hoehn-Saric, R., Nash, E. and Stone, A. (1966) Therapist empathy, genuineness and warmth and patient therapeutic outcome. *Journal of Consulting Psychology*, 30: 395–401.

Turner, R.H. (1962) Role taking: process versus conformity. In: *Human Behavior and Social Processes*. Ed. Rose, A.M. Boston: Houghton Mifflin. pp. 20–40.

Tyrer, P. (1991) Neuroses and personality disorders. In: *Concepts of Mental Disorder: A Continuing Debate*. Eds Kerry, A. and McClelland, H. London: Gaskell.

von Bertalanffy, L. (1973) *General Systems Theory: Conditions, Developments, Applications*. New York: Georhe Braziller.

Weiss, R.S. (1991) The attachment bond in childhood and adulthood. In: *Attachment Across the Life Cycle*. Eds Parkes, C.M., Stevenson Hinde, J. and Morris, P. London: Routledge.

Wilkins, P. (1997) *Personal and Professional Development for Counsellors*. London: Sage.

World Health Organisation (1992) *The ICD-10 Classification of Mental and Behavioural Disorders*. Geneva: WHO.

Index

abuse, suffered by clients, 15, 30
alexithymia, 47
ambivalence, of clients, 90, 142
assessment for counselling, 19, 44–64,
    71–2, 72–3, 76
attachment, and later expectations,
    16–17
attendance, 81

borderline personality organization
    (BPO), 142–5
breaks in counselling, 81
brief counselling, 77, 78

care/caring
    capacity for, 11
    obstacles to providing, 19–20
    obstacles to seeking, 15, 18–19
    professional and personal, 17–18
clarification, 128
    of goals, 88–91
    of symptoms, 47
clients
    contextual influences of, 127–32
    difficulty in receiving help, 15,
        18–19
    expectations of, 9, 12, 15, 19
    psychosocial support for, 75–7, 85,
        97, 127–32
    role of, vii, 12, 18, 52, 55, 72,
        88–9
    in straightforward transactions, 5
closed systems, 33
competence of therapist, 78

complicated transactions, viii, 4,
    5–6
    basic interaction patterns and,
        30
    predicting, 44, 46, 48, 50–1, 51–7,
        61, 62, 63
complicating influences
    clarification of, 128
    constraint of, 129, 130–1
concern, absence of in client, 50–1
confidentiality, 75, 141–2
context of counselling transactions,
    32–43, 122–33
contract for therapy, 93–6
coping, 73, 95
counselling transactions, vii, 2–14
    context of, 32–43, 122–33
    criteria for straightforward
        transactions, 5–6
    distortion of, 20, 23, 31
    monitoring, ix
    safety of, 57–60
    see also complicated transactions;
        straightforward transactions
counsellors see therapists
criminal justice system, working with,
    139–42

deep disclosure, 55–7
defensiveness, 53
delays in referral, 68–9
demands of systems, 34
    competing, 33–4, 36, 39
depression, 47

discussion, 124
disclosure of personal information,
    51–7, 90

emotional climate, 25, 55
emotional disposition of therapist,
    departures from, 60–2, 104–9,
    110–11
emotions, 9–10, 29
    containing, 50, 53, 111
    inability to register, 47
empathy, 29, 42, 95, 114
endings *see* termination
expectations, 7, 9, 43, 66
    of clients, 9, 12, 15, 19
    early attachments and, 16–17
    of therapists, 73

family background, disclosure about,
    52–5
family relationships, 11–12, 31
family system, 33, 34, 39
family therapy, 77, 80
first interviews, 72–4
formulation of interaction pattern,
    112–19

goals of counselling transactions, 4, 5,
    9, 34, 35, 36, 39
    clarification of, 88–91
    renegotiation of, 91–2
goals of systems, 34–5, 36, 38, 39, 43
group therapy, 77, 79

healthcare system, working with,
    135–9
healthy privacy, 56
help *see* care/caring
hierarchy of systems, 37–9

idealization, 56–7
information
    about therapist, 72–3, 74
    for clients, 81–2
    disclosure of, 51–7, 90
    validation of, 69–70, 71
insurance for therapists, 78–9

integrity of systems, 36–7
interaction, 1, 2–3
    levels of, vii–viii, 6–10
    patterns of, 25–30, 102, 104, 112–19,
        120–1
    see also personal level interactions;
        public level interactions
interpersonal difficulties, 136, 142
inter-related systems, 40–2
interventions, 86–101, 112–20
interviews, 72–4
    for assessment, 45–6, 61
intuition, 10
involvement
    of clients' support network,
        127–32
    of other professionals, 75, 95, 96–7,
        126–7
isomorphism, 40–2

labels for clients, vi, 1, 14
learning disabilities, 47
limit-setting, 92–6
long-term counselling, 77

mixed dominance, 25, 28–30, 110
mode of referral, 71–2
monitoring personal reactions, 60–3
multiple assessment interviews, 45–6,
    61
multiple problems, 51, 90

neglect, suffered by clients, 15, 30,
    53

obligation to counsel, 73, 124
omissions of information, 53
open systems, 33
overlapping systems, 39–40

past interactions, influence of, 15–31
personal goals, 35, 36
personal information, disclosure of,
    51–7, 90
personal level dominance, 20, 24, 25,
    26, 28
    shift towards, 107–9

personal level interactions, viii, ix,
6–10, 14, 15, 19, 36–7, 64
constraining, 119–20
enhancing, 114–19
goals of, 35
personal therapy, 125
personality disorders, 135–9
presentation of problem, 7, 46–8
presenting 'of' themselves, 52, 64,
143
problems
past 53
presentation of, 7, 46–7
responsibility for, 48–50, 89
professional style, 9, 23
departures from, 104–9, 111
and 'ordinary clients', 23–5
professional training, 125
promotion of therapy, 129–32
psychopathic disorders, 140–2
psychosocial adjustment, deterioration
in, 73
psychosocial environment, 66
psychosocial support for clients, 75–7,
85, 97, 127–32
psychotherapy system, 142–5
public goals, 35–6
public level dominance, 21, 23, 25,
26–8
shift towards, 104–7, 110
public level interactions, vii–viii, 6–10,
14, 15, 19, 35, 61–2, 64, 92
public-personal disequilibrium, 50, 62,
63
public-personal equilibrium, 20
of client, 110
shift in, 19, 20–1, 23–5, 31, 64
of therapist, 19, 86, 99, 101, 102–21

questionnaires, 72

reactions of therapists, 110, 111,
118–19, 121
monitoring, 56, 60–3
record keeping, 79
referral, 65–72, 126–7
rejection of clients, 75–6, 82–3

relationships, past, 11–12, 31
disclosure of 52–5
repression, 145
resistance to personal disclosure, 90
responsibility for problems, 48–9,
89
risk assessment, 57–60, 77
role
of client, vii, 12, 18, 52, 55, 72, 89
of counsellor, 9, 12, 88–9
role-taking, past interactions and,
16–20
roles, vii
clarification of, 88–91
person and, 10–13, 14, 15
preserving, 86–101

safety of counselling transactions,
57–60, 79
second opinions, 80
self-esteem, low, 57, 190
self-evaluation, 44
self-hatred, 57
self-injury, 48, 57
self-referrals, 69–70, 71
separations, 54
shared clients, 144–5
short interventions, 114
significant figures, 54
skills, 8, 9, 10
splitting, 145
straightforward transactions, viii, 4–5,
9–10, 25, 51–2, 63–4
departures from, viii-ix, 5–6, 14, 18,
23, 31, 45, 47, 61, 62, 71
subsidiary goals, 34, 35
sub-systems, 36
goals of, 35
supervision, 60, 104, 111, 113, 118,
124–5
support for therapy, from client's
family, 129–30
support from other professionals, 73–4,
75–6, 80–1
systems, 32–4
of counselling transactions, 34–7
systems theory, 36–43

taking stock, 110–12
telephone referrals, 70, 71
termination, 9, 81, 83–4, 85, 97, 99, 127,
    132
therapists
  contextual influences of, 122–7
  information about, 72–3, 74
  perception about client, 12
  personal reactions of, 60–3, 110, 111,
      118–19, 121
  professional style of, 23–5
  role of, 9, 12, 88–9
  security of, 79–80
  in straightforward transaction, 5

time-limited therapy, 84
training for therapists, 125
transaction window, 6, 21–3, 104
transfers, 81, 126–7

untoward events, 75–7
usual practice, deviation from, 67

vagueness of symptoms, 46–7
validation of information, 69–70, 71
violence, 48, 50, 58
  risk of, 58–60

written material for referral, 71–2